Reconstructing communicating: Looking to a future

LEA's COMMUNICATION SERIES
Jennings Bryant / Dolf Zillmann, General Editors

Selected titles in Communication Theory and Methodology
Subseries (Jennings Bryant, series advisor) include:

Ellis • Crafting Society: Ethnicity, Class, and Communication
Theory

Greene • Message Production: Advances in Communication
Theory

Heath/Bryant • Human Communication Theory and Research:
Concepts, Contexts, and Challenges

Olson • Hollywood Planet: Global Media and the Competitive
Advantage of Narrative Transparency

Perry • American Pragmatism and Communication Research

Riffe/Lacy/Fico • Analyzing Media Messages: Using Quantitative
Content Analysis in Research

Salwen/Stacks • An Integrated Approach to Communication
Theory and Research

For a complete list of titles in LEA's Communication Series, please
contact Lawrence Erlbaum Associates, Publishers

Reconstructing communicating:
Looking to a future

Robyn Penman
Communication Research Institute of Australia

LAWRENCE ERLBAUM ASSOCIATES, PUBLISHERS
2000   Mahwah, New Jersey   London

Lawrence Erlbaum Associates, Inc., Publishers
10 Industrial Avenue
Mahwah, NJ 07430

Cover design by Kathryn Houghtaling Lacey

Library of Congress Cataloging-in-Publication Data

Penman, Robyn.
Reconstructing communicating : looking to a future / Robyn Penman.
  p. cm.
Includes bibliographical references and index.
ISBN 0-8058-3648-9 (alk. paper)
1. Interpersonal communication. 2. Communication—Study and teaching. I. Title.
BF637.C45 P435   2000
302.2—dc21
                                                            00-039395
                                                            CIP

Books published by Lawrence Erlbaum Associates are printed on acid-free paper, and their bindings are chosen for strength and durability.

Printed in the United States of America
10 9 8 7 6 5 4 3 2 1

Contents

⟨⟨◯ Acknowledgments

For me, this book is an important closure point—albeit only temporary—in a long journey of inquiry into how we can understand communicating and what it can mean to engage in research in it. However, as with all forms of inquiry, this has been a socially constructed effort. I have maintained sustained conversations with some conversational partners over years and distances, and they have contributed substantially: Barnett Pearce has offered much in the way of constructive constructionism and encouragement, and John Shotter has kept on pointing me to new ways. Others have offered significant interventions and opportunities at very needful moments and I thank them: Eero Riikonnen for his therapeutic insights and good Finnish sense; Bob Craig for trying to keep me from "going overboard"; all the members of the Redwood Gang for inspiring me to continue; the Alta dialogue group for their challenges; and, of course, my colleagues at the Communication Research Institute of Australia for all of our explorations in matters of practice. Maureen MacKenzie-Taylor, Barnett Pearce, David Rogers, Sallyann Roth, Art Shulman, and Sue Turnbull all provided valuable suggestions on various drafts of this manuscript and I very much thank them for their contributions and support. I also need to acknowledge that chapter 5 of this book first appeared in *Communication Theory* (1992) and has been reproduced here, although with some modifications and extensions.

1

Communicating matters

This book is about the practice of communicating, and how we make sense of it, while still in the process of communicating. This book is also about the quality of our communicating practices and how we make judgments about them—also while communicating.

I first began my conceptual exploration of these issues with a seemingly innocent and obvious question: "What makes a good relationship?" It soon became apparent, at least to me, that this question needed to be reworded to "What makes a good communication process?" Communication is the observable practice of a relationship, and so it was to the actual process of communicating that I had to attend. In all the research and conceptual work that followed, the question of what can make a good communication process has been my central preoccupation.

This exploration was challenged and extended when I took up my role as a foundation director of an independent, nonprofit communication research institute. The institute's primary charter is to improve the quality of communication practices in society—through research, practical advice, training, and public forums on important issues. Although our charter appears rather grandiose and presumptuous, it is nevertheless the driving force behind our activities. In engaging in these activities since 1985, I have repeatedly found that mainstream communication studies and understandings have had little to offer. Indeed, I have been confronted with problems and challenges that rarely, if at all, get mentioned in the mainstream journals.

I take the opportunity later in this book to draw on many of the practical research projects in which I have been involved. But for the moment, consider the challenge of how you would go about developing, structuring, and writing government legislation so that ordinary citizens can actually read, understand, and use it. For me, this became a challenge as to how I could reconceive and reconstruct legislation to emulate conversational practices. Alternatively, consider the problem as originally conceived, of how to educate HIV/AIDS patients about triple combination therapies and how to ensure treatment compliance. This became a challenge of to how to talk from within the lived experience of HIV/AIDS patients and provide "conversational" moments appropriate to their information needs. As a further contrast, consider the problem of how to ensure that the general aviation industry followed safe aviation practices. My challenge here was to make sense of what the people in the industry needed to understand in order to engage in safe practices in a very competitive economic environment.

All of these challenges I faced are important and practical, and all were met by the application of a particular communication point of view: one that takes the activity of communicating as the prime focus of concern. This book is about what happens when you do this very thing and say that communicating matters. This book reconstructs the process of communicating—hence its title—and explores future possibilities for practical work in communicating. The starting point for this reconstruction process is a particular imagining of what we can take communicating to be.

⟪ Imagining communicating

What are we researching and teaching about communication, and what is it we are talking about in everyday life, let alone doing? This is not a simple, academic matter of definition that beset the field of communication from the 1960s to the 1970s, but instead a practically important one of what is possible and what is not. The way in which we conceive of communication sets the constraints on what we study and what we don't; on what ways we use communication to act in our world and what ways we don't; and on how we communicate and how we don't. As Wittgenstein (1953) reminded us, what we haven't imagined in language is not brought about in life, and what we cannot speak about is bound to remain unsaid. I think these two sides of the coin are equally important. What we can imagine brings a particular form of life into being and simultaneously precludes other forms of life from being.

In the everyday world of organizations in which I usually work, the imaginings about communication are taken very much for granted. Members of these organizations usually present their concerns to me as centered on the need to improve communication, or to resolve some problem of communication. They expect that this can be done in a straightforward, technical manner. What they want to do is "get their message across better", "improve the information flow from the top down" or make sure that "others comply with their instructions." These requests reflect a certain imagining of communication that is predominant in our society and that by its very imagining precludes other possibilities from being. In this common imagining, communication is a relatively straightforward activity that we use to achieve effects—sending messages or controlling others. In this imagining, communication is merely an instrumental activity.

I'm sure that many of you will recognize this imagining as what is commonly referred to in our literature as the transmission view of communication. I'm also sure many of you will say but that is just "old hat", at least in the communication literature. However, let me assure you that it is extraordinarily alive and well in the everyday public domain. It is an imagining I must continually work with, albeit not in. I confess, that I've always been a little amazed, or at least bemused, by the capacity of so many people to dismiss the complexities and messiness of communication and treat it as a straightforward, success-without-effort process. Although there is no doubt that communication often seems to be an effortless process—especially because it is one we engage in constantly—it is also one in which the norm is misunderstanding, not understanding (whatever that may be). Nevertheless, the contemporary imagining persists. As such, it is believed that little effort needs to be expended to ensure that goals of understanding, or the like, are met.

Although I continue to express amazement at this imagining, I should know better. This contemporary imagining, or conception, of communication is firmly rooted in a 3 century-old tradition of modernity that simply will not let us see other possibilities. I explore the effects of this tradition in greater depth in the next chapter. Here, however, we need to recognize how well entrenched the contemporary imagining of communication is and how difficult it will be to construct another one.

In 1999 I had occasion to reflect on the entrenchment of the contemporary imagining while on a panel of past presidents celebrating the 20th anniversary of the Australian & New Zealand Communication Association at its annual conference (Penman, 1999). In contemplating my own involvement in the field over those 20 years, I realized two significant points. The first was that I have been pursuing the challenge of what it can mean to understand the actual process of communicating over all those years and in a range of contexts. The second was that in engaging in this pursuit, I have found myself frequently marginalized among fellow communication scholars—although certainly not all. It was as if I was concerned with something else apart from what is commonly called "communication studies." Well, in a significant way I was, and still am.

To make my point here, I want to distinguish between two approaches to the idea of communication as a field of study, recognizing that it is an over-simplification and one that I redress in the next chapter. In the first approach, there is the communication studies that takes communication as a site, or topic, in which something far more interesting than communication per se usually takes place. From my view of the field, this is the most common approach. Communication studies is a site available for the application of multi-disciplinary tools to ask a whole range of questions about anything other than communicating. The study of culture within communication studies is a good case in point. For example, Larry Grossberg (1993), a leading contributor to cultural studies, remarked that communication studies is no more than an institutional home for cultural studies. More bluntly, Wiley (1995) portrayed communication studies as merely a "detour" for cultural studies. The study of health communication is another case in point. In that field, you can find a whole range of studies employing the disciplinary tools of psychology to study such things as communication campaigns. This is most notable in those studies that use the theoretical assumptions and models associated with the construct of attitude. The key point here is that in neither of these subfields is the actual process of communicating taken to matter. As I show further in the next chapter, this reflects the entrenched Enlightenment view of the immateriality of communication.

In contrast, there is the communication studies that takes the process of communication itself as the concern, not as the mere carrier or site for something else. This approach to communication studies is premised on the belief that communicating matters and in such a way that other disciplinary tools are not relevant. Stuart Sigman (1995) wrote about this as the study of "communication consequentiality." Consequentiality leads to a consideration of the procedures, the dynamics and the structures of communicating, not of the effects (consequences). Sigman (1995) made the following contrasts that help to highlight the differences I am addressing here:

- If you imagine that the process of communication makes no difference in the meanings generated in mass, organizational, interpersonal, or other contexts, then communicating is not worthy of study.
- If you imagine that meaning is determined by freestanding cognitive processes, linguistic patterns, social structures, cultural codes, and the like, then communication is merely a neutral vehicle for that conveyance and is only worthy of study through the disciplines that have already demarcated the constructs of cognition, culture, and the like.
- If you imagine that the meaning that emerges from each and every communicative moment cannot be predicated on social, structural, or psychological features, then you must turn your attention to the determining force played by the very process of communicating.

It is the last imagining that I am taking up here, and for very good, practical reasons. Put bluntly, I believe that the contemporary imagining of communication is not serving us well (if it ever did). It is a conception of communication that focuses on the individuals and, thus, pushes the notion of community aside; that focuses on the end effect and, thus, ignores the means; and that presumes the possibility of certainty and, thus, denies the open-ended creativity of communication. It is also a conception of communication that ill-befits us for the postmodern age. According to Toulmin (1990), we are poised on the brink of change that leaves us with only two choices: either to face the future, and so ask about the future options open to us, or backing into the future with no horizons or possibilities before us, simply the clutching at nostalgia. This book is about facing the future—a future in which the possibilities in new understandings of communicating open up new options for us. However, to explore these possibilities we need to take a great leap from where we are now to where we could be in the future.

✆ A discontinuous leap into a different realm

For the past two decades, there have been clear signs of a general transform-ation underway in the humanities and social sciences based on the recog-nition of the role communication plays in constructing our lives (e.g., Craig, 1993; Gergen, 1982; Harré, 1986; Leeds–Hurwitz, 1995; Pearce, 1995; Pearce & Cronen, 1980; Shotter, 1984). It is in the field of communication that the core of this transformation could take place. However, it seems to me that if we are to take up this possibility, we may need to make a discontinuous leap from where the field is today if it is to get somewhere else in the future. I am deliberately using the term *discontinuous* here to emphasise that I am not going to be exploring an extension of our mainstream understanding of communication but something else entirely, something outside of our tradition of modernity.

Yet, even in making this claim, I am mindful of Richard Bernstein's (1992) caution about the slippery and vague nature of the terms *modernity* and *post-modernity*. His resolution was to use the term *modern/postmodern* to reflect a mood: "one which is amorphous, protean, and shifting but which nevertheless exerts a powerful influence on the ways in which we think, act, and exper-ience" (1992, p. 11). My use of the phrase *discontinuous leap* needs also to be taken in this way. It is meant to reflect a new mood that is more than an exten-sion of the old. I suspect that we will only be able to judge the extent of the discontinuity after we move forward with it and have a chance for later retrospection. So, for now, I invite you to leap with me and see where we get.

Craig (1999) in his paper on "Communication Theory as a Field" showed one of the possible consequences of this leap: a reconstruction of the field of communication within a practical discipline. Craig proposed that, in order to achieve his vision, the constitutive model of communication be taken as a metamodel. This constitutive model recognizes the consequentiality of communication (Sigman, 1995) and acknowledges communication itself as a fundamental mode of explanation (Deetz, 1994). For Craig (1999), recognizing the consequentiality of communication and acknowledging its constitutive nature are the hallmarks of genuine communication theory. So, by leaping into this new mood, in which communicating matters, we are able to explore what genuine communication theory can be.

To undertake this exploration requires us to inquire into communicating and not communication; to treat communicating as the essential problematic of concern; and to recognize that we construct our reality in our communicating. I make this discontinuous leap here by treating these three notions as serious and exploring what it can mean for us living our lives in communicating and for us, in particular, as inquirers into this process of which we are a part. How is this understanding of communicating different? What intellectual baggage must we give up? How can we actually study communicating in this new view? What could it mean? Perhaps most important, why would we want to? These are the basic questions that I explore.

However, by virtue of the very discontinuous leap I am making, the offerings to these questions cannot be in the conventional "rationalist/empiricist" mode. There are no unambiguous answers to be given, and there are no generalizable solutions to be found. In engaging with my explorations here you will need to exorcise what Bernstein (1992) called the "Cartesian anxiety": the anxiety that unless we can discover fixed, unassailable foundations we will be surrounded by intellectual and moral chaos. Saul's (1992) passionate and devastating account of the "dictatorship of reason in the West" points profoundly to this need to discard the frantic search of answers, to step away from "the narrowing effect of a civilization that seeks automatically to divide through answers when our desperate need is to unify . . . through questions" (Saul, 1992, p. 585). So instead of seeking the definitive answers, I want to explore new "constellations" (using Bernstein's sense, 1992), create new "horizons" (using Toulmin's sense, 1990) and ask new questions (as Saul, 1992. pleads for). I welcome you to join me in this exploration.

But this exploration will not be into the world of theory per se, and certainly not into that abstract realm of pure theory. Rather, it is an exploration into the practice of communicating. What I am concerned with here is practical knowledge, not theoretical, because I want to be able to generate understandings of, and in, communicating that allow me to do things in it— things that can benefit society, and things that can improve the quality of communicating in society.

James Scott (1998) provided an absorbing, and tragic, account of the consequences of neglecting practical knowledge in his book, subtitled "How Certain Schemes to Improve the Human Condition Have Failed." The schemes he described included the Great Leap Forward in China, collectivization in Russia, and compulsory villagization in Tanzania, Mozambique, and Ethiopia— all of which "are among the great human tragedies of the twentieth century, in terms of both lives lost and lives irretrievably disrupted" (Scott, 1998, p. 3). Scott identified a combination of four critical elements to account for why such well-intended schemes went tragically awry. One of these critical elements is a "high-modernist ideology" reflected in an extreme self-confidence in scientific and technical progress: an ideology we can also find in comparable communication schemes to improve (or should it be control?) the human condition.

In contrast, Scott made the case for "the indispensable role of practical knowledge, informal processes, and improvisation in the face of unpredictability" (Scott, 1998, p. 6). In developing his concept of practical knowledge, Scott drew on the Greek concept of metis: a wide array of practical skills and acquired intelligence in responding to a constantly changing natural and human environment. Although I make recourse to more familiar Aristotelian concepts of knowledge in later chapters, this concept of metis is still pertinent to matters of communicating, as Scott (1998) himself noted. Most important here is the way in which metis works. Scott illustrated this with the work of Red Adair in capping oil well-head fires:

> Adair's job cannot, by definition, be reduced to routine. He must begin with the unpredictable—an accident, a fire—and then devise the techniques and equipment (from an existing repertoire , to be sure, but one invented largely by him) required to extinguish that fire and cap that well. (Scott, 1998, p. 314)

Metis, then, is not the application of a set of universally applicable, technical rules, but instead is the development and application of specific procedures appropriate to a specific situation. As I proceed, I hope to show that what Red Adair does with well-head fires, we need to do with communicating issues: begin with the unpredictable, and then devise techniques to change it. I shall be parallelling Scott's arguments for the indispensable role of practical knowledge, informal processes, and improvization in the face of unpredictability when dealing with matters of communicating.

✺ The reconstruction process

The central theme throughout this book is concerned with what constitutes good communicating and, concomitantly, good communication research. However, in exploring this central theme, I have a twofold purpose. First, in keeping with the vision of Craig (1999), I want to reconstruct a practical theory of communicating that establishes the possibility for a genuine disciplinary base. This is the primary focus of the first half of the book. Second, I want to show what it can mean to undertake research, or practical inquiry, in communicating, once we have reconstructed it. That is the focus of the latter part of the book.

The exploration into the possibility of a practical theory begins, in the next chapter, by looking at the social and historical context in which we have come to understand communication and then proceeds to consider three options for how we can view communicating when looking to a future. For me, this consideration of context is critical in that it helps our understanding of how and why we find ourselves where we are in the field of communication studies today. At the same time, it reflects the very historically and culturally context-ualized nature of communicating itself.

In the third chapter, I turn to a consideration of what it can mean to treat communicating as the process of concern. Here I voice my particular social constructionist view of communicating, in terms of talking about language as something we inhabit, and consider how we make sense in this inherently vague, ambiguous, and uncertain process. What this means for a practical theory of communicating is also considered. Finally, in chapter 3 I explain why I have been using the term *communicating* and not *communication*, as part of a shift into a new language game.

When we start to use *communicating* seriously in this new language game, we are led into quite a different realm. This realm is described in the fourth chapter, where I explore a notion of practical knowledge—akin to metis—and its relationship with the lived experience of communicating. This exploration becomes rather awesome for, not only do I overturn our convent-ional understandings of knowledge and truth, but I then go on to a reconsider-ation of morality and aesthetics. As I warn you at the beginning of chapter 4, this is truly "work that is not for the timid" (Cronen, 1995a, p. 224). At the best it could be described as audacious, although I can almost hear some voices crying "how presumptuous." Nevertheless, the reconstruing of the classic questions of truth, beauty, and goodness was called forth from the arguments leading up to chapter 4.

When we recover experience and take communicating as the process of concern, we need to ask questions that include the moral and aesthetic realms. In chapter 5 the moral question is put to the process of communicat-ing. There I directly address the central theme of the book: "What can it mean to say that it is good communicating? How can we make judgments of the process?" Chapter 5 is, in large part, a reproduction of an article that appeared in *Communication Theory* (Penman, 1992) but it is so central to the major thrust of the book that I had to include it here.

The sixth chapter, on dialogue, is pivotal: It both describes an exemplary form of good communicating according to the criteria developed in chapter 5 and sets up the basis for the practical inquiry methods and tools developed in the three chapters that follow it. At the outset, it is important to understand that I use this notion of dialogue in a particular, prescriptive way; one that identifies "features of contact, that are not always present, may not always be desirable, and are not always possible, but than can serve as an ideal toward which communication may fruitfully move" (Stewart & Zediker, 1999, p. 6).

In chapter 7, I turn to issues of practical inquiry in and of communicating by asking the questions: "What research is possible? What could it be like? What could it accomplish?" I take the exemplary form of dialogue as the basis for considering one form of research practice, although not the only one possible. This form occurs in what I call the "primary research position." It is from this position that we can directly face the practical issues in our world and, from the position of participation, ask: "What can we do?"

The example of Red Adair I gave earlier illustrates this form of primary research: one that begins with unpredictability, and requires the use of practical knowledge in informal processes. As Scott (1998) pointed out about Red Adair, the primary researcher must devise specific techniques for each specific situation, albeit from an existing repertoire also devised by the researcher. Chapter 8 describes the main tools in my repertoire that I have used in conducting primary research, as well as some tools from other people's repertoires that have the potential for application in specific communicating research situations. One of the tools I describe there consists of the practice of "telling of": a more informal conversational style of talking/writing than that usually used in academic literature. This informal conversational style is the one I have deliberately adopted in writing this book. It is far more appropriate to the spirit of my arguments than any removed, objective style.

In the last chapter I attempt to provide some good closure by pulling together a number of the arguments and showing how the tools of practical inquiry into communicating can be used. I draw on two disparate case studies to do so: one concerned with understanding the conditions for dialogue, and the other concerned with how to talk from within the lived experiences of HIV/AIDS patients—one of the examples I gave at the beginning of this chapter. From these case studies, I point to several key factors in conducting inquiries in our daily lives: the need to avoid the search for the solution, and the importance of asking questions in good faith.

This book begins with the central theme of what constitutes good communicating and, concomitantly, good communication research. This theme is addressed throughout the book, but by the end it will become twin themes of acting in good faith with our ways of morally knowing. These intertwined concepts provide us with the necessary radical departure (or discontinuous leap) from the rationalist's quest for truth and scientific knowledge. In departing from the rationalist's quest into the one to be undertaken here, we find ourselves face to face with our humanity where it matters—in communicating.

2

Understanding context

Whenever we engage in conversation with another, we draw on many different features of the conversation in our sense-generating process. One of these features is the context. Where is the conversation taking place, under what circumstances, with what history? However, context is not a passive thing lying there in the background, a mere surrounding to the presumed more important text. On the contrary, context exists in a reflexive relationship with the utterances or text. In this sense, "context returns to its original Latin source as a verb meaning to weave together. Thus context and utterance reflexively evolve and inform one another" (Cronen, 1995a, p. 225).

In the more complex sense in which context is taken in its verb form, meaning is generated from the mutual interplay of context and utterance. Our understanding of communication, and in communicating, is contextually bound. Recognizing this interdependency between context and utterance inexorably leads to the recognition that all knowing is generated in context; specifically, in the context of communicating.

We—you, the reader, and I, the writer—are engaged in a sense-generating process out of the contexts of our reading and writing. However, we are in a curious, multiply layered and, hopefully, overlapping set of contexts. As a contribution to our disembodied engagement, I want to offer the context as I see it for generating a new sense of communicating—the new sense that relies on the discontinuous leap I talked about in chapter 1.

There are two important dimensions to understanding this context: the contemporary context of where we are now, and the historical context that brought us to this point. In this chapter I first develop a sketch of the contemporary scene, both within the field of communication and more broadly across the humanities and social sciences. Then I turn to the historical context. I have found my own explorations of this historical context extremely important in understanding where we are now and, most important, in understanding the intellectual containment of that history. Finally, I turn to face the future by asking what choices we have before us.

৻ৣ Contemporary context and challenges

The field of communication studies today could perhaps best be described as diverse, and in more ways than one. A good illustration of this can be found in the collection of articles in two of the 1993 issues of the *Journal of Communication* on "The Future of the Field—Between Fragmentation and Cohesion".

Although the questions addressed in these two issues are primarily from an American point of view (42 out of the 48 papers), they are nonetheless questions and challenges currently facing all who teach and research in the area of communication. The central thrust of all the questions and challenges is the disciplinary status of the field of communication. For an area of study to be a discipline, teachers and researchers in the field would share a common understanding of what they were studying and researching, and students in the field would finish their degree with a set of understandings and methods that would distinguish them from say a sociologist or psychologist. If a communication degree or research program has nothing distinctive to offer, then its *raison d'être* is open to question.

Although most authors in the 1993 issue agreed, or assumed, that communication is not (yet) a discipline, the pathways to disciplinary status and the importance of having it varied. Some of the authors were concerned that the field of communication has no substantial core of knowledge or any unified theory (e.g., Beniger, 1993; Rosengren, 1993) and that it will not progress until the core of knowledge builds up and theory is unified. Central to the argument of other papers is the proposition that the most important thing to advance the field is to address the real, practical problems of the communicative world (e.g., Avery & Eadie, 1993; Docherty, Morrison & Tracey, 1993). A third group drew on particular areas of knowledge to suggest new directions and challenges, especially in the area of mass communication (e.g., Gomery, 1993; Livingstone, 1993).

The multitude of arguments and approaches, in themselves, demonstrate that there is no unified field or agreed-on core of knowledge, and make it difficult to see any coherence at all. It is, as Brenda Dervin described it, "as if we are all studying a very large elephant. Without addressing the question directly, we seem to assume that we are studying the same elephant, while comfortably relegating ourselves to our own parts" (Dervin, 1993, p. 45).

What makes this situation truly problematic is that it is not even the same elephant! Indeed, it would seem that there are three very different elephants represented by what the authors take communication to be. I return to the specific natures of these different "elephants" at the end of this chapter. For the moment, I want to describe one of these elephants—perhaps currently the smallest one but the one with the greatest potential, and certainly the most different. This is the elephant that is trumpeting the challenge to the main herd: the challenge to recognize the role that communicating plays in constructing our lives.

The challenge from within

It is not possible, or necessary, to systematically document all the challenges from within the field of communication. Since its formalization as a field (in terms of academic departments) there have always been dissenters from the mainstream. For my purposes here, I focus on the most recent challenges only. These recent challenges were foregrounded in a two-part forum on "Social Approaches to Communication" published in Communication Theory in 1992 and assembled into a larger collection by Wendy Leeds-Hurwitz in 1995. As Bob Craig noted in his forward to the book, Social Approaches to Communication, it "should mark a turning point in the development of interpersonal commun-ication research" (1995, p. v).

Although the chapters in Leeds-Hurwitz's (1995) book reflect quite a diverse collection, they all share in common a rejection of what has been called the objectivist position. Loosely speaking, we can describe the objectivist posi-tion as one that seeks an understanding of communication outside of the communication process, one that adheres to a quantitative, empirical approach for explaining (not necessarily understanding) communication—or, at least, the outcomes of communication.

In the introductory chapter to the collection, Wendy Leeds-Hurwitz (1995) identified 11 themes that reflect these social approaches and that by counterpoint indicate the challenges. Here I take the liberty of drawing on her good thematic work, with thanks and acknowledgment, albeit with some rearrangement.

First, social approaches are challenging the very focus of study and what we take communication to be. Rather than describing outcomes of a process, studying the process from an individual's point of view, or making inferences about what goes on in the mind of an interactant, social approaches focus on the very process itself. Social approaches are, by their very name, social. Communication is not taken to be a mere mechanical or technical process; it is more complex and inherently interactional.

Second, social approaches are challenging what it is that we take to be the "site" of knowledge. Rather than assuming that our reality exists independent of human activity, some version of the social construction of reality is assumed (Berger & Luckman, 1967). As such, the old methods of inquiry relying on scientific method are also being challenged. Research takes on new meanings and new methods in social approaches. A concern with these new meanings and new methods is explored at length in following chapters.

Third, the central concern of social approaches is how meanings are created out of interaction. This is a challenge to the assumption that humans are passive beings acting out a set of preexisting rules. Instead humans are seen as more or less active agents, capable of doing new things, and of making new rules as well as breaking them. This third theme also challenges the assumption that meanings reside in the words themselves. Instead, it is in the process of active humans interacting that meaning is generated.

Fourth, social approaches recognize, as I did at the start of this chapter, the critical role of context, particularly cultural. Interactions do not take place in a neutral or value-free void; rather, they are bound with their context. Again, this has direct implications for methods of study that challenge the classic scientific method. In particular, if context is critical, then it it is not possible to adopt an objective, neutral stance.

Fifth, social approaches are both holistic and reflexive. These approaches recognize the need to study the whole of interaction—to understand how all the contributions are related, including that of the researcher. In these approaches, the researcher is in a reflexive relationship with the other participants in the interaction. This is in stark contrast to the assumption that researchers can be neutral, objective, and outside of the process they are studying.

The broader contemporary challenge

As Craig (1993) and Davis and Jasinski (1993) pointed out in the same issue of the *Journal of Communication* I introduced earlier, confusion in the field of communication reflects a broader transformation in the humanities and the social sciences. This broader transformation reflects substantial changes in ways of thinking about social practices—changes radical enough that some have claimed a paradigm shift from the "modern" to the "postmodern" (e.g., Bernstein, 1983; Lyotard, 1984; Toulmin, 1982).

However, the notion of postmodern has been used in many different ways, from an application of a new style of architecture and the development of the city state to anything that is new or avant–garde. It is clear that not all arguments with the label "postmodern" are the same. For some, postmodern is a state, whereas for others it reflects a change in understanding social processes. Second, not all postmodern arguments have genuinely abandoned the assumptions of modernity. Bernstein (1992) well recognized the slipperiness of the term *postmodern* and has opted for the more inclusive *modernity/postmodernity*. Similarly, in Toulmin's (1990) later work, he preferred to call this current transformation *the third stage of modernity*.

Whatever term we take, what I am concerned with here is a particular transformation in ways of thinking about social practices, a transformation that orientates us towards process. This transformation has two major, interwoven threads that act as challenges to the mainstream: One is a challenge to our methods of discovery and the other is a challenge to the features of the social world that are taken to be important.

When we focus specifically on the social sciences, the traditional assumptions of a behavioristic, causal model of humans are rejected in favor of ones that take humans to be active agents, more or less in control of their own lives. These alternative assumptions in turn lead to the rejection of conventional experimental models for understanding human actions (e.g., Harré & Secord, 1972; Shotter, 1975)—much as has been described with the social approaches to communication—and a call to generate new means of discovery. Along with this is a change of focus to the joint activity between human beings (i.e., humans communicating) as being at the core of our social knowledge (e.g., Gergen, 1982, 1985; Harré, 1986; Shotter, 1984, 1993). Today, the challenges across the social sciences are broadly centred around talk of "social construction"—talk that has been used to explore such notions as identity (e.g., Shotter & Gergen, 1989) and memory (e.g., Middleton & Edwards, 1990), as well as communication per se (e.g., Pearce & Cronen, 1980).

At a more philosophical level, there has been a major challenge to the notion of objectivism, well documented in Bernstein's (1983) book *Beyond Objectivism and Relativism*. Here, the challenge is to the assumption that there can be some permanent, ahistorical foundation to which we can ultimately appeal in determining the nature of truth or knowledge (see also Rorty, 1980). This rejection of the possibility of objectivism arises from a consideration of the impossibility of separating our knowing what is out there from us, the knower. In other words, it once again comes from a recognition of the socially constructed nature of our world. Along with the challenge to objectivism, has been a challenge to the notion of neutrality/rationality, and Bernstein again captures the flavour of many of these arguments in his later work *The New Constellation* (1993). There, he drew attention to a recurrent constellation of ideas that have at their heart an ethical-political concern with praxis (action). In later chapters I too explore this ethical-political concern with praxis, as it relates to the practice of communicating.

Many other philosophers of this century and earlier made contributions to the challenges briefly described here and there are occasions when I return to them in greater depth. My major concern now is simply to sketch some of the contemporary challenges as a way of framing the next exploration into our historical legacies. What are these contemporary challenges challenging? How is it that these challenges are being made now?

✒ Historical legacies to be exorcised

From the description of the field of communication given earlier, I have suggested that it is very fragmented in its concerns and its approaches. And, although some aspects of the field (e.g., rhetoric) were never dominated by the ideas that I have challenged, the majority of approaches do share a common historical legacy. It is a denouncement of this historical legacy that is at the heart of the contemporary challenges. To understand this legacy we need to go back in time to the dawn of the Enlightenment in the 17th century. It was then that the foundations for the past 3 centuries of modernity, as well as our mainstream conceptions of communication and research methods, were laid.

The rationalist heritage

Toulmin's (1990) historical analysis of the rise (and fall) of modernity showed how much the founders of modernity strove to remove themselves from their time and their humanity. The major contributor to this movement, Descartes, was convinced that we could build a secure, permanent body of human knowledge using rationally validated methods that relied on working from formal logic, with general principles and abstract axioms. Toulmin argued that this provided the basis for "the deeper meaning of the term 'scientific method' " (Toulmin, 1990, p. 81). Scientific method was developed to generate pure, context-free, and universal truths.

However, these moves didn't just happen in a vacuum, out of context. They were made for very good reasons at the time. Toulmin's (1990) explorations suggested that during the period 1610 to 1650, three critical events took place that drove the search for pure reason. One was the death of Henry Navarre in France in 1610 which heralded the start of a bloody 30-year war throughout Europe. This both reflected and accompanied enormous religious conflict between Protestants and Catholics which initiated the second critical event, the Reformation. At the same time, the traditional cosmology of the sun and planets moving around a stable stationary Earth came under sustained attack—making the third critical event. In the light of these events, the rationalists' program of change was both daring and desperate, reflecting a great need to strive for certainty in a very uncertain world.

In order to be able to pursue the context-free questions of Cartesian rationalism, the philosophers of the day made four major moves (Toulmin, 1990). First, they shifted from the oral to the written. With this shift, public arguments before audiences became unacceptable as a means for discovery or confirmation. The new program of philosophy rejected all issues to do with argumentation among particular people in given circumstances and about specific topics. Indeed, the very notion of rhetoric was deprecated. As I discuss shortly when I turn to John Locke, the 17th-century philosophers were at pains to dismiss the use of rhetoric because it "thereby mislead the judgment; and so indeed are perfect cheat" (Locke, 1997, p. 452). Even today the word *rhetoric* is often still used in this deprecatory way.

So, instead of using rhetorical devices, the soundness or validity of an argument could only be demonstrated as a series of written chains of statements with internal consistency. Things had to be proved in writing. To quote Toulmin, "formal logic was in, rhetoric was out" (1990, p. 31). It is obvious that this valorization of the written word and the written means of proving is still paramount in our scholarly activities today. You need only look to all the scholarly journals we have to demonstrate this. But perhaps an even more striking example of this valorization is an observation I have frequently made at conferences. There is often a scholar standing in front of an audience, talking about communication, and saying "What I do in this paper is . . ." or "in the first part of this paper . . ." Even in talk these scholars refer to the written mode.

The second move made by the 17th-century philosophers was from the particular to the universal. Prior to this move, theologians and philosophers handled moral issues on a case-by-case basis, following the procedures recommended by Aristotle in the *Nichomachean Ethics*: "Sound moral [judgment] always respects the circumstances of specific kinds of cases" (Toulmin, 1990, p. 32). However, with this second move, it was no longer acceptable to explore the implications of specific cases; instead all examination had to be based on comprehensive, universal principles of general theory by which particulars could be rationally linked together. With this shift, casuistry as a means of making moral judgments got the same disparaging treatment as did rhetoric as a means for making arguments. Again, there are obvious legacies seen today. For me, among the more notable are the codes of practice for such communication professionals as public relations practitioners and journalists. Such codes are typically laid out as general principles, without consideration of specific contexts and cases.

In the third move, the philosophers went from the local to the general. The ethnographic, geographic and historical sources used by the 16th-century humanists were discarded as irrelevant to true philosophical inquiry. As Toulmin noted, Descartes confessed to a youthful fascination with these sources, but overcame them: "History is like foreign travel. It broadens the mind, but it does not deepen it" (Toulmin, 1990, p. 33). Descartes argued that philosophical understanding never comes from the accumulated experiences with a range of local and specific cases. Instead, philosophy has to find the general principles by which all the particulars could be connected. So, in rejecting the local, contextual sources, a whole realm of context-related questions became irrelevant. Instead, the goal was to develop abstract, generalized axioms to cover all manner of things, regardless of context.

Fourth, they turned from the timely to the timeless. Questions about the timeliness of decisions, actions, and utterances had been central to earlier philosophy, especially as it hinged around matters of jurisprudence. However, with this fourth move, concern with transient human affairs was put into second place. The concern was not with factors that held good in different ways at different times, but instead with the timeless principles that held good at all times in all places, outside of the context of time. With this fourth move, I hope you can see how the very process of communication was dismissed—it being the most timely and transient of all human affairs.

These four moves are reflected in the conventional empirical methods still used in some arenas of communication today (e.g., see the journal *Human Communication Research*). They are particularly reflected in the objectivist, empirical approaches that the social approaches are challenging. However, before exploring this in more detail, we need to turn our attention to another historical legacy—one that is directly related to our concern with communication.

The legacy of John Locke and the empiricists

The pursuers of context-free and universal truths, however, had a problem—language (or communication, in a broader sense). This problem can best be seen in the arguments of the British scholars who heralded the start of the empiricist school and whose arguments still influence many areas of communication research today. The core of their arguments rested on the proposition that there was a great division between the material and the immaterial, and only material things mattered. The rational principles had to be applied solely in relation to the material, not the immaterial. In this great division, communication was classed as inessential or immaterial—it did not count (Shepherd, 1993).

Those British scholars of the 17th century had to class communication among the immaterial in order to maintain their other arguments regarding logical processes and the need for certainty of knowing. The linguistic radicals in particular, found abhorrent the conception of language as an ever-moving stream, a medium of innovation, and a source of great uncertainty (Davies, 1987). They could not build a secure, permanent body of human knowledge using rationally validated methods that relied on working from formal logic, applying general principles and abstract axioms, with something as uncertain as ordinary human language.

For example, in the *Leviathan* Hobbes urged that people had to purge language of all ambiguity, expel metaphor, outlaw new phrasings and reduce language to a rational system of signs. Wilkins, a compatriot of Hobbes, went even further. He argued that natural languages were just too treacherous to be tolerated—the meanings kept on changing and betraying the speaker/listener. Wilkins wanted to destroy the very nature of language in which words referred to things other than themselves, and make the words the things themselves. Making the words the things themselves would ensure understanding, eliminate contention, and guarantee that the pathway to pure knowledge was achievable (Davies, 1987).

Fortunately they could not quite achieve the destruction of natural language, nor eliminate the inherent uncertainties of communication. But they did the next best thing: They asserted it did not matter. The search for pure knowledge would go on by asserting that language (and by implication communication) was irrelevant to the search; words did not count. We have the heritage of that view in such contemporary phrases as "actions speak louder than words" and the childhood saying of "sticks and stones will break my bones but names will never hurt me" (although, curiously, that saying was usually uttered in my childhood just when the words *did* hurt).

However these linguistic radicals were merely forerunners to the main work that sealed the fate of communication for 3 centuries. A number of recent scholars have pointed to the writings of John Locke as the direct source of our current conception of communication (e.g., Copleston, 1985; Peters, 1989; Spano, 1993). Indeed, it was Locke who coined the term *communication* in the way it is still popularly used today. So why and how did he do this?

To understand the role ascribed by Locke to communication, we need to start with his *Essay Concerning Human Understanding* (1690/1997). His primary concern in this essay was to examine the mind's capacity and what objects our understandings were, or were not, fitted to deal with. He thought that we needed to confine our philosophical attention to matters that fell within the scope of human intellect in order to make progress in knowledge.

The foundational unit for Locke's treatise on understanding was the idea, and these ideas were derived from sensation or reflection. In other words, all our ideas are grounded in experience—the basic empiricist principle.

However, this is not to imply that ideas are simply passively received into the mind—this is only the case for what Locke calls simple ideas. Complex ideas, on the other hand, are actively framed within the mind.

But ideas are private things and humans are, according to Locke, social beings. So how do ideas get from one mind to another? They get there via signs. To be social beings, we need "sensible and public signs" to signify the ideas in our minds. These sensible and public signs are our words. For Locke, words stood for nothing but the ideas in the mind of the person who used them. However, he wrote: "To make words serviceable to the end of communication, it is necessary (as has been said) that they excite, in the hearer, exactly the same idea, they stand for in the mind of the speaker" (Locke, 1997, p. 426).

There are two significant points I want to make of this proposal here. First, Locke never intended to write about words or language: "When I first began this discourse of the understanding [sic], and a good while after, I had not the least thought, that any consideration of words was at all necessary to it " (Locke, 1997, p. 435). However, he felt drawn to do so in order to account for the relationship between ideas in our heads and the extent and certainty of our knowledge. For Locke, the latter had a close connection with words, because words interpose themselves, "like a medium" between ideas and knowledge (p. 435). However, in giving this account of knowledge, it became quite clear that not only were words subservient to ideas, but language was subservient to knowledge. Language and words were merely tools for other things. Indeed, in Locke's view it was possible to have thought without language (Parkinson, 1977).

Second, Locke was very concerned about what he saw as the "imperfection" of language, especially when used in conversational or rhetorical ways. For him, ordinary language use, such as in conversations or persuasive language, as he took rhetoric to be, corrupted ideas: "All the art of rhetoric . . . are for nothing else but to insinuate wrong ideas, move the passions, and thereby mislead the judgment; and so indeed are perfect cheat" (Locke, 1997, p. 452). What was needed was a special, more refined, use of language that did not corrupt ideas: "Speech being the great bond that holds society together, and the common conduit, whereby the improvements of knowledge are conveyed from one man, and one generation to another, it would well deserve our most serious thoughts, to consider what remedies are to be found [for rhetorical abuse]" (p. 453).

What is important about Locke's deliberation in this regard is that it was the first time—in writing, at least—that the word *communication* was used for other than physical conveyance of matter or energy. With Locke, the term *communication* "begins its long shift from matter to mind, from physical to mental sharing . . . to construct a theory of society in which thoughts are conveyed with as little corruption from language as possible" (Peters, 1989, p. 394).

I think most of you will recognize this as the commonsense view of communication used in our everyday contemporary life and to which I made reference in chapter 1. This is the conduit (Reddy, 1979), or transmission, view of communication that presumes that the process is a simple means of conveying ideas between people or, to quote the common catch-phrase, of "getting your message across." It is a view that is still reflected in much of modern-day communication studies: that communication is merely a trivial vehicle for something far more important. Pearce and Cronen (1980) described this received view as one in which communication is construed as a colorless, odorless vehicle of thought that works best by getting out of the way.

Let's turn to what made this idea possible. What conditions were proposed that allowed Locke to develop this particular conception of communication? What conditions still maintain this particular imagining of communication in our contemporary society?

Central to Locke's theory of understanding and the concomitant development of the theory and practice of liberalism is the presumption of a major gap between the individual and society, between the public and private spheres. To quote Peters (1989, p. 387): "This fundamental and rarely acknowledged division defines the condition in which 'communication' can be *imagined*" (his words, my emphasis). In other words, Locke's and our current everyday conception of communication can only exist, as it were, by presuming a fundamental division between the individual and society. There would be no need for imagining communication as the means for transferring ideas from one mind to another if we did not believe in the notion of separable and independent minds.

For the moment, though, let's hold onto Locke's imagining and explore what form of life it sustains; particularly what form of community life. To do this we need to turn to Locke's later work on political theory, his *Treatise of Civil Government* (cited in Copleston, 1985). In this treatise, he started with the belief that all people are naturally in the state of nature and remain so until they consent to make themselves members of a society. This starting premise is in accord with his presumption that there is a great divide between individuals and society.

So why would individuals want to form societies? This was the core question Locke had to address and justify. His major argument was that "individuals consent to submit to the will of the majority in order to enjoy their liberties more securely" (Copleston, 1985, p. 133). In other words, communities are created in order to protect the individuals and their property. Communities, as with communication, are backdrops to the sovereign individuals and their property/ideas.

In Locke's world view, there is no role for debate or discussion in the public sphere, in the community. Indeed, there is no public process at all for the forming of the will of the majority. Instead, because we can only conceive of meanings and understanding in the control of human minds, a majority is simply when more than half hold the same ideas in their minds. As a consequence, community opinions are simply the majority collective of individual ideas.

In this form of social life, conflict and incommensurability are removed from the public realm—from the community—and placed in the private experiences of individuals. This was important for Locke. He wanted to ensure that what notion of the public sphere there could be was confined to matters of science and reason, not politics and morality. He believed that, in a civil society, people reasoned through their ideas rationally, in a scientific manner; they did not or should not generate their ideas out of public conversations.

We live with Locke's inheritance today. A key part of this inheritance "is the sacrifice of theoretical coherence about the creation of public worlds (of community) on the altar of individual freedom" (Peters, 1989, p. 396). Locke's imaginings did not allow community to come to the fore, only the individual. In the same way, his imagining treated communication only as a background mechanism for linking the ideas of one person to another.

We can see the legacy of this imagining about communication and community in a whole range of current political/public communication practices. Here, I deliberately use Locke's notion of communication, because it is still the most predominant imagining in public life today. To illustrate this, I draw on two studies of political communication done by the Communication Research Institute of Australia (Penman, 1990). In both studies, we interviewed some of the key players in public/political communication processes—

senior members of the party then in government, and senior public servants in charge of public information activities. Three major themes were identified from our interviews.

First, we identified an economic/marketing frame for talking about communication processes. We particularly recorded frequent reference to the metaphor of "selling ideas." This belief was further reinforced by the employment of marketing and advertising agencies to do the "selling." In essence, the players believed that political ideas and policies need to be advertised and sold to citizens as if they were consumers of ideas. As one participant put it, political ideas "can be sold like cat food."

Second, concomitant with the growth in the use of market research and advertising agencies is the growing reliance on experts, with three major effects. First, the increasing use of these experts, rather than giving politicians and public servants a real understanding of the electorate, acts to keep the citizens out of the political discursive space. Second, as Habermas (1971) pointed out, the use of these experts has led to politics being scientized, with the application of their methodologies replacing the processes of public opinion formation. Third, as both Habermas (1971) and Gadamer (1975) noted, with the use of these technical experts, we have lost our orientation to human questions (see the earlier discussion of the Rationalist heritage); what remains is an exclusively technical perspective.

Third, the technical perspective goes hand in hand with a view of communication as a mere tool for achieving political/public effects. The view that policies had to be sold to the public and the political party is indicative of this view of communication-as-a-tool, as is the belief that the number of broch-ures picked up, or the number of press releases made into articles, is indicative of communication success.

Together, these themes show the legacy of Locke's imagining in all those practices that presume that political ideas need to be sold to citizens via well-managed communication campaigns. In turn, these practices presume that members of society are nothing more than simple consumers of political ideas, available for manipulation by social science experts. The individual is still sovereign and communication is still simply a means for conveying political ideas, but now we have the added twist that technical experts are needed to measure and manipulate these ideas.

However, there are other imaginings possible, ones with quite different consequences for the future. We do have alternatives open to us that can lead to a different sense of communicating and community. These alternatives, though, require a profound philosophical change.

◖ Looking to the future

Shepherd (1993) suggested that communication scholars have three choices to the traditional assumption that communication is inessential whereas other things are essential: They can continue to accept the assumption that communication is inessential or immaterial; they can reject the assumption of a division between essential and inessential altogether; or they can deny that communication is inessential and, conversely, assert that it does matter. When the articles in the two review issues of the *Journal of Communication* (1993) are re-read in the light of Shepherd's three choices, their seeming disparity and fragmentation makes sense, because each author or group of authors have, however implicitly, chosen one of the three options. Although it may be possible to construe further choices, Shepherd's three options seem to account for the current choices that have been made.

The most popular choice has been to accept the conventional wisdom of the past 3 centuries: that communication is immaterial, nothing more than a vehicle for conveying ideas. This choice is reflected in arguments about the need to investigate how messages can be best "shaped" and manipulated in order to best "transmit" the ideas they "contain", and to bring about desired effects on others (Penman, 1988). Arguments such as these are the corner-stones for the political views on communication I described at the end of the previous section. As well, arguments such as these reflect a choice for what Krippendorff (1993) called *message-driven research*—research that focuses on the messages (words or texts) and their effects. It is also a choice for under-taking research that will lead to generalized, abstract, and context-free know-ledge.

Arguments like Grunig's (1993) and Herbst's (1993) that presuppose the possibility of a grand theory of public relations or public opinion and what it could offer the field of communication, exemplify this approach. As Krippendorff argued, it is likely to remain a popular choice because "People in positions of authority are all too eager to embrace deterministic reality constructions that can offer them the prospect of forcing predictability and controllability onto others" (1993, p. 40).

However, one consequence of accepting the common wisdom is that there can be no discipline of communication per se. If communication is immaterial and merely a conveyance for ideas, then there is no discipline to develop—how could you have a disciplinary study of nothing? Instead you are only left with other disciplines (e.g., psychology and English) competing or collaborating over the "site" (Kavoori & Gurevitch, 1993) or "topic" (Peters, 1993) of communication.

A second and more socially important consequence of making this first choice is that it leaves us with a very impoverished conception of communication that limits the options open to us (Penman, 1988). There are at least four core problems that contribute to this impoverished view. First, people are seen as separate from their activities; in particular, people are separate from the critical activity of meaning generation. Meanings are in the word packages we send to others and, provided that the package arrives unsullied, the meaning put in will be the meaning taken out. Second, the actions (or behaviors) of the people in the process are taken as separate contiguous events—a message is sent and then received—implying not only some notion of linear causality, but also a mechanistic model. Third, the active doings of people are taken as simply a product or effect, with no concern for the process of the doings. Fourth, the contextual nature of the whole process is denied; when the focus is on the effect, the historical embeddedness of the process is ignored.

Reddy (1979), in his extraordinarily insightful analysis of the conduit metaphor underlying the view of communication in this first choice, clearly documented the massive social pathology arising from this view of communication. Included in the social pathology is a trivializing not only of the process of communication but of the other participants in it—a trivializing of any sense of human connection. This is the same trivializing that I described in Locke's account, earlier in this chapter. Most important, this conduit metaphor and its trivializing turns communication into a success-without-effort process.

The second choice open to us is to reject the conventional wisdom and the basic division between material and immaterial. This is the antidisciplinary approach that Shepherd equates directly with Rorty's (1980) anti-foundational arguments. In his arguments, Rorty sought to directly undermine and deconstruct what he called the "Cartesian-Lockean-Kantian tradition" and, in doing so, to reject philosophy as a foundational discipline. Rorty's arguments reject all materiality and embrace everything as immaterial; they are arguments that reflect an extreme relativist's position. With these arguments, communication is everything and nothing.

There are serious problems associated with this second choice. First, as Bernstein (1983) maintained, a relativist position still resides in the Cartesian world of dualism, of the either/or. Relativism is simply the antithesis to objectivism. So this is a choice of contrast, or of reaction to the Cartesian foundationalism. It is not a choice that offers a genuine alternative, outside the Cartesian frame.

Second, accepting a view of communication along with everything else as immaterial is to celebrate the insignificance of being itself (Shepherd, 1993). In such a celebration, notions of good or right are replaced with an amoral stance of anything goes, if it works. I am very much reminded here of Feyerabend's earlier argument (1975) against method, where he claimed that the only principle that does not inhibit progress is "anything goes". Rorty, following Feyerabend, was also a critic of the very idea of method and in favor of "anything goes", particularly if it keeps the conversation going. Although I am also very much concerned with keeping the conversation going, I agree with Bernstein (1992) that Rorty failed to realize that his rhetoric tends to close off the conversation, rather than open it. Most important, as Bernstein (1992) noted, Rorty's rhetorical strategies do nothing towards the struggle to "articulate, defend and justify one's vision of a just and good society" (p. 253); they lead, as I said earlier, to an amoral stance.

The third choice is to deny the conventional wisdom and assert that communication is material. It is only this choice that offers the possibility of a disciplinary view, one that says communication is foundational to our being (Sless, 1981). It is material and does matter. Although this goes against the last 3 centuries of mainstream philosophical tradition, it is a view that nevertheless has had its own advocates for centuries (e.g., Vico, 1988, but writing in the 1700s). These arguments about the materiality of communication are now coming to the fore, as reflected in the general transformation in the humanities and social sciences I described earlier in this chapter. It is important to understand that this third choice is not a direct reaction to either or both of the other two choices. Whereas relativism (the second choice) is simply the antithesis to objectivism (the first choice), the third choice is discontinuous with both. Yet, in a curious way, it can be seen to incorporate both of the other choices. By taking communication as material, we end up realizing that all choices are choices as to how we take communication to be.

One of the important consequences of making this third choice is its implications for practice. When communication is taken as material, we can begin to recognize the critical role it plays in our understanding of the world in which we live. Even when we are theorizing about communication we are engaged in its practice (Craig, 1993; Pearce & Cronen, 1980; Penman, 1992). This enables us to directly face the practical problems of our world and to ask, from the position of participation, what we can do. It also enables us to engage in the struggle that Bernstein (1992) referred to: of articulating, defending, and supporting one's vision of a just and good society.

It is the third choice that I have made, and that guides my writing here. So let us turn to elaborate on the implications of this third choice. What can it mean if we treat communication as material? What can it mean to take it as the focus of our concern, not as the mere carrier for something else? And, how does it allow us to develop and defend a vision of a just and good society?

3

Communicating in a different game

In looking into the particular future I want to project here, we need first to reject both Locke's basic premise that individuals and their ideas are the primary unit, and the presumption of a great divide between the private and the public. These imaginings of Locke deny any sense of participation, and any sense of genuine community and, concomitantly, trivialize the process of communicating.

I realise that the dominance of rationalism and empiricism over the past 3 centuries may make any alternative imagining hard. This dominance makes it seem utterly self-obvious that our world is populated by individuals defined by the boundaries of their physical skin and with minds that contain ideas. Indeed, the sense of our bodies as containers (for minds, ideas, thoughts, etc.) is such a dominant root metaphor in the English language that it is hard to conceive otherwise (Lakoff & Johnson, 1980). Yet, if we are going to move forward with our third choice, we are going to have to discard that view.

As an alternative, we need to imagine that the basic human reality is not individual people, but instead people in conversation (Harré, 1983). With the start of such an imagining the great gap between the individual and society, between the private and public spheres, dissolves. Indeed, no gap is presumed.

Instead, the fundamental starting point is one of relating, of communicating.

Heidegger's arguments are useful here to help this imagining along. He started his deliberations by pointing to what he believed was a false starting point in Cartesian arguments. From that Cartesian position, the person is first and foremost an isolated thinker employing reason to objectively derive knowledge. This is captured in Descarte's famous Latin motto, *cogito ergo sum* (I think, therefore I am). In contrast, Heidegger argued we are "first and foremost a situated interpreter, understander, or 'sense maker' engaged in everyday coping [and] as situated interpreter the person is irreducibly relational not individual, social not psychological" (Stewart, 1995, pp. 26–7). For Heidegger, the primary human reality was being in the world—being engaged with others.

Similar arguments can be found in the pragmatic philosophy tradition founded by Dewey (1981) and I will introduce these at various points as I proceed. They can also be found in the newer arguments of the social constructionists (e.g., Gergen, 1982; Harré, 1986; Pearce, 1995; Penman, 1992; Shotter, 1993). The implications of these arguments for construing communicating in a different game are also discussed in this chapter. However, please bear in mind that there is no one single approach to social constructionism. In Barnett Pearce's guide to social constructionists (1995), he pointed out that social constructionism falls within Bernstein's (1992) notion of a "constellation": It is a collection of different voices that understand each other sufficiently to go on together. In what follows is my voice in this constellation.

᭙ Being in language

Let us start by considering what it can mean to be in the world and, particularly, to be in language. There are various ways in which we can explore this and I draw on two different threads: one developmental and the other from philosophy of language.

Becoming human

Earlier considerations of child development created a picture of a child passing through a series of developmental stage that resulted from a learning or experiential process. In that view, language was something children acquired. In contrast, work of the past 3 decades points directly to a picture of children emerging through language, as it were. There is extensive observational work showing that well before infants can talk, the patterns of caregiver–infant interaction are conversational ones (e.g., Bruner, 1975; Lock, 1978; Snow, 1977).

From their day of birth, infants become part of a social milieu through conversational processes. From the very start, caregivers treat their infants as if their behavior meant something and the infants can understand—even if only in a very primitive way. Caregivers normally don't just silently pick up their young infant and hold her/him, they murmur words like "There, there." They also continually offer labels for behavior like "Oh, are you feeling hungry little one? Do you want some milk?" Usually, these labels imply intentions on the part of the infant, like "Oh you really just wanted a cuddle, didn't you?" Even when caregivers are not making coherent utterances they spend their interactional time with their infants uttering nonsense words and phrases setting up all the basic interactional processes for the infants to fit into.

It is this very assumption by the caregivers—that their infants are persons requiring talk—that brings them into "personhood", and into social life (Shotter, 1978). By treating infants as if they were humans, they become so. Most important here, however, is the recognition that infants begin life in a personal relationship, one created in, among other things, the caregiver's talking. It is through being in this language that infants begin to take on their own life and become humans.

As Vygotsky (1978) described it, all of the functions we acquire as children appear on two planes, first among people as an *interpsychological* (or inter-mental) category and later as an *intrapsychological* (or intramental) category. It is only after children have practiced in conversation that they are able to become conscious of it or control it in any way. It is this interpsychological category of Vygotsky's that is most important here, because it is in the interpsychological that communicating takes place.

We can see the primacy of the interpsychological in children's acquisition of written language skills. Children read aloud, talking the words, well before they read silently. Indeed, as Ryle (1963) noted, the trick of talking to oneself in silence is acquired slowly and with a great deal of effort—it is nothing that occurs naturally. For us to be able to read silently we have had to go through a long process of talking sensibly aloud both as we read and as we talked with other people. I think this is a very important observation that is more often than not overlooked: that, developmentally, talking and reading aloud is first.

Not only can we see this developmental process with each child, we can also see it over human history. It was not until the Middle Ages that people learned to read without reading aloud (Ryle, 1963). Before that time, all reading was talking aloud. And before that time, it was also thought possible that you could write, or at least copy marks on paper, with no understanding at all—as if the words were independent of understanding (Goody, 1986). In considering this long historical development process, I wonder how it could have been possible to have any intrapsychological concepts at all? But it was, and we do—we are inundated with intrapsychological concepts. Of course, one of the most notable and pervasive of these intrapsychological concepts centers on the conduit metaphor of communication.

Inhabiting language

Such considerations as childhood development and longer-term historical development of humans have generated a powerful tradition in the philosophy of language centered around such people as Gilbert Ryle (1963) and Ludwig Wittgenstein (1953). For both of these authors, it was only the intermental or interpsychological use of language that mattered. Indeed, they argued that much of our vocabulary of mentalistic terms (e.g., *belief, idea, memory*) had no internal referent at all: that is, the concepts do not exist. The belief, idea, or memory is not literally in our head, but instead in our talk about it. This, of course, is in stark contrast with the arguments of John Locke that I discussed in chapter 2. In Locke's view (1997), the idea comes first, in our heads, and then we use words to stand for the idea.

Wittgenstein, perhaps more than any other contemporary philosopher, undertook extensive investigations into the role of language in communicating, and it is to him I turn now. As most other authors who have written about Wittgenstein comment, he is not easy to read or understand. In part, this is because he wrote about language in two very different ways. In his first set of explorations, he described language mainly in terms of a representational role, or as providing pictures of things in the world. However, as Janik and Toulmin (1973) pointed out, he also came to realize that the relationship between language and the outside world was ineffable. The very nature of language does not allow us to directly represent aspects of the world.

In his second set of writings, the *Philosophical Investigations* (1953), Wittgenstein approached the role of language in a different way. This different way is proving invaluable to our constructionist understandings of the world as well as, unfortunately, contributing to the difficulty of understanding Wittgenstein. In the *Investigations,* Wittgenstein used language to explore what language can be and, in doing so, pushed the limits of possibilities and simultaneously exposed language's inherent ambiguities and uncertainties.

One of the key contributions in this second set of writings is the notion of a language game, or of playing in speech. Wittgenstein introduced this concept of a language game, to "bring into prominence the fact that the speaking of language is part of an activity or form of life" (1953, p. 11). It is not the words themselves that have meaning, but the way in which we use them in the context of their use. As Shotter (1993) remarked, words are best thought of as having no predetermined meanings but instead as being the means for use in the making of meanings—they are like tools whose significance is brought about in their use.

If words have no meaning independent of the context of use, then language cannot be used to directly represent the world, or as John Locke would argue, our ideas about it. Instead, language-in-use directly acts to create our world. It is in language that we bring about the world as we know it. In other words, it is our language used in context that generates knowledge. Even recognizing this, as Shotter (1993) pointed out, it may still seem as if words are used to represent things. However, if this does seem to be so, it is only because "representation" is one of the many uses for our language in sustaining a particular form of life. Given this, I can readily concur with such propositions as those of Potter and Litton (1985), that language is constitutive of what it represents. In using language we are bringing about what it is we are trying to represent.

Shotter (1993) noted another significant contribution of Wittgenstein's philosophy. Everyday language use appears vague and ambiguous, because it really is vague and ambiguous. Our activities, or descriptions of them, are not vague because we have not yet discovered their underlying nature, instead they are vague because there is no underlying pre-determined order to be discovered. This vagueness and ambiguity is, of course, the very thing the linguistic radicals of the 17th century abhorred. Although, in their very abhorrence they were giving recognition to the existence of what they abhorred, their solution was to purge language of these qualities. Here, in contrast, I am recognizing these characteristics as inherent, and I am celebrating them.

It is important perhaps to reemphasize here, that the way in which I am using the concept of language is radically different to the way imagined by Locke and used in our contemporary everyday understandings. Stewart (1995) pointed to the critical difference: We are not talking about language as the system of rules described by Saussure or about a system of sending signals to indicate ideas in the minds of individuals as captured in the conduit metaphor; instead, we are talking about language as something we inhabit (Gadamer, 1992). Our being-in-conversation is being-in-the-world; alternatively, our being-in-the-world is being-in-conversation. Our understandings of the world emerge out of this conversation, not out of deciphering a set of linguistic signals standing for ideas. In this view, language as a medium that separates people from reality is discarded in favor of language as something we live in, jointly.

Implications

There are two important implications of this understanding of being-in-language. First, if there is no direct, or isomorphic, relation between our physical experience of the world and our understanding/talking about it, then it is not possible to adopt an objective position for studying that world. Our understandings arise out of meaning generation processes, not out of our physical experiences or observations per se. Once we discard the possibility of objectivity, we must also discard the traditional objective–subjective distinction. Without a notion of objectivity, the comparison with subjectivity becomes meaningless (Harré, 1983). Within the imagining being developed here, there is only one realm—the intersubjective—for researcher and researched alike. Note that by *intersubjective* I am referring to all that goes on between people, or all that people do jointly.

The second, and related, implication is the recognition that all accounts and explanations generated in our research process are not discoveries of the external world, but instead are inventions of the intersubjective. Knowledge does not have an objective, immutable base in the "real" world—it is not out there to be found or discovered. Instead, knowledge is created in the human social realm. This equates with Rorty's (1989) proposition about the contingency of language: truth is made in language, not found. Of particular significance to communication scholars, is the recognition that our understandings of communicating generated through our talking and research is conducted within, and by, the very same process we are seeking to understand. In generating theory and describing action, we are doing no more than creating a story to make sense of our world (Rorty, 1980; Shotter, 1987).

It is perhaps important to emphasize here that neither of these implications are meant to suggest that in language is all that there is. That would be to fall into the absolute relativist's trap. Rather, I am only saying that all that we know is in language. There could well be some non-linguistic reality outside of our linguistic knowing, but our language-bound human nature does not allow us to kno it. It certainly doesn't allow me to write of it here.

⸎ Making sense in communicating

Acting willfully and jointly

How can we see ourselves in this being-in-language? What stories can we construct to make sense of how we act into language? And how do we understand what it is we do? One important element is the assumption that our actions in communication have a voluntary base. We enter into communication more or less willfully, as agents of our own lives (Harré, 1979). This does not mean that our actions are totally free of environmental constraints or that we have total free will. It simply means that our actions are not wholly determined by our immediate environment or anything like internal causations. Rather than seeing communication as consisting of behavioral responses to stimulus messages and thus explicable by natural laws, communicative action is seen as understandable on the basis of a series of voluntary actions.

What is important about this is that I am denying any mechanistic account of how I act the way I do. I am denying that something out there has control over me (e.g., "She made me do it"). I am equally denying that something inside has control (e.g., "It was an unconscious impulse"). I am able to deny these things because I accept that language is constitutive. On the other hand, I also have to recognize that being-in-language means I am being-with-others. So, although I am an agent, more or less, I am also in conversation with someone else who is an agent, more or less. This is where the fun starts and where the truly challenging nature of communicating becomes more obvious. Let me start to build a picture of this conjoint process.

What we need to start with is a conception of communicating, "which consists only in the flow of activity between people, not in the sequential occurrence of things; in a process, not in a series of products" (Shotter, 1986, p. 205). In acting into this process we find ourselves in a rather more difficult (but also more exciting) place than conventionally conceived. It is not so much that we enter the process of communicating to follow a predetermined plan; rather we find ourselves acting into and specifying the process we are in, jointly. In this sense, communicating becomes a self-specifying activity, because our jointly enacted past activities point to the directions of our current ones.

We are neither in nor out of control of the process, but mutually contribute to it. Even though it is a conjoint process, as persons in the process we are able to move in more than one way at any particular time. As Dewey said, one of the aspects of being uniquely human is the ability to respond in several ways to an "impulse" (Cronen & Lang, 1994). Dewey's words can seem a little odd some 80 years later. By impulse we can take it to suggest that when we are moved by certain things—such as the actions of our conversational partner—we always have more than one option open to us. This variability open to us is reflected in the voluntary decisions we make on how to proceed.

Given this voluntary base, our capacity to generalize about communication is very limited; both as participants in the process and as researchers in another process. Macintyre very astutely pointed to the human base of this limitation:

> We are thus involved in a world in which we are simultaneously trying to render the rest of society predictable and ourselves unpredictable, to devise generalizations which will capture the behaviour of others and to cast our own behavior into forms which will elude the generalizations which others frame (Macintyre, 1985, p. 104).

With this element about acting willfully and jointly, I have discarded certain ways of making sense in and of communicating. I have abandoned the explanatory constructs of causality and any mechanistic account of behavior. I have also discarded attempts at generalization and prediction. In contrast, I have suggested that, as people entering the communication process with others, we do so in willful ways, yet without any individual capacity for pre-determination. Once we enter jointly with another in the process it takes on a life of its own, as it were, something beyond the worlds of both causality and individual action. In joint action we create a wonderfully uncertain and often mysterious (Pearce, 1989) communicating process. The amazing beauty of it all is that somehow we usually manage to go on. But how?

Understanding as we proceed

Given that our understanding of the world is generated in communicating, and that this is a process occurring over time, it follows that the temporal context makes a major contribution to our understanding. What we determine to be knowledge and how we interpret communicative action is a function of the historical context in which the process takes place. As the context changes, so to does our understanding. Just as important, without the context there can be no intelligibility of communicative action (MacIntyre, 1985). What we do only makes sense in context. This is the very same point I made earlier in discussing Wittgenstein's (1953) argument about language.

However, the very temporality of understanding negates the possibility of a stable knowledge base. If you think about what happens in ordinary conversations, this makes some sense. In ordinary conversations we often say to ourselves, "Oh, she means that" and then, as the conversation proceeds over time, we often find ourself saying "Oh, she didn't mean that, she meant this." As the context of the conversation, including the temporal one, changes, so too does our understanding. David Sless poignantly captured this momentary, changing nature of understanding: "Understanding is the dead spot in our struggle for meaning: it is the momentary pause, the stillness before incomprehension continues .... Thus understanding is a temporary state of closure" (Sless, 1986, p. i).

This momentary pause, or elusive moment of interaction, is where it is all at and I return to it again in later chapters. However, let us ask here, how do we know that we understand? What does it mean to say that we have understood? These questions are particularly interesting ones when any notion of intramental concepts are outside the story frame. We cannot say we know we understand because the idea is now in our head, nor can we say we know we understand because you and I share the same idea. (Where do we share it? What does it look like? What could it represent?) So how do we know?

We know for the moment and we know because we are able to go on. In other words, we know or understand because we are able to keep on going in the conversation. Shotter (1993) said that this is one of the important things about Wittgenstein's investigations: He was not concerned with anything mysterious going on in our heads, but instead with simply going on with each other. Wittgenstein suggested to "try not to think of understanding as a 'mental process' at all"; instead, simply ask "in what kind of circumstances, do we say 'Now I can go on'" (1953, no. 154). Knowing how to go on includes how to relate to others in the future, and in what contexts it may be appropriate to act in that way (Cronen & Lang, 1994).

Trying to imagine this notion of understanding can be difficult. We have developed such an intramental set of terms and concepts to describe meaning, knowledge, and understanding that it is often difficult to relocate these in the momentary understandings between people. Sometimes I find it helps to imagine a good conversation, one on which all participants can easily go on, as akin to a good dance. Although in this instance it can only be particular kind of dances: those whose performance relies on the co-ordinated action between partners (such as ballroom dancing). With each step that the partners take in co-ordination with each other, the dance moves forward. Each partner is able to go on with the other when each moves in ways that enables that progress. That the dance goes on shows that moments of understanding have occurred. Pearce and Cronen also point to the importance of this notion of co-ordination in their theory on the "Co-ordinated Management of Meaning" (e.g., 1980). For them, *co-ordination* refers to an irreducible element of human life: We are inextricably connected in a complex pattern of relationships through which we move. The ways in which we manage these complex patterns of relating generate meaning.

What is the relation between theory and practice?

This picture of understanding that I am developing here has an important implication for what we do as researchers, academics, or students of communicating. Whatever stories, or higher blown theories, we propose of communicating helps to bring about the very phenomena we are proposing. In generating ways to make sense of our communicative world, we are in fact providing the framework for understanding and acting in it. The range and nature of our possibilities for action are as broad or as narrow as the range and nature of interpretations/theories available. With this assumption, an integral link between theory and practice becomes apparent.

But there are different types of theories, or accounts, and thus different types of links. In chapter 2, I made reference to various scholars who were passionately concerned with the need to build a grand, unified theory of communication (e.g., Beniger, 1993; Rosengren, 1993). This notion of theory reflects closely the moves to modernity described by Toulmin (1990)—to universal, general, and timeless accounts—and that he earlier called the "received view" of theory (Toulmin, 1974). John Shotter described this way of theory as:

> the urge i) to bring a unity to things, ii) in terms of a belief, supposition, hypothesis, or theory, iii) formulated in terms of a small set of hierarchically related formal elements, iv) thought of as representing states of reality, v) which can be cognitively manipulated to produce other representations of logically possible states. (Shotter, 1997a, p. 2)

Although recognized as one of many possible ways of constructing understandings, this type of urge, and the theory it generates, offer very little option for action. It is so far removed from our practices that it is unable to inform them, let alone open up new possibilities. Accounts of this theoretical form are irrelevant for practice. What I am concerned with here is a practical theory.

John Shotter introduced this notion of practical theory in his book *Social Accountability and Selfhood* (1984) and Vern Cronen built on it in his contribution to *Social Approaches to Communication* (1995a). Cronen (1995a) proposed five features of a practical theory.

Practical theory:

1. is concerned with everyday life practice
2. provides an evolving grammar, or way of talking about, communicative practices
3. generates a family of methods for the study of situated social action
4. co-evolves with both the abilities of its practitioners and the consequences of its use
5. is assessed by its consequences—specifically in terms of how it makes human life better.

Craig and Tracy (1995) have also argued for a grounded practical theory of communication. Within their perspective, theory is seen as a "rational reconstruction of practices for the purposes of informing further practice and reflection" (p. 248). More recently, Bob Craig (1999) built on this proposal in his essay, "Reconstructing Communication Theory as a Dialogical-Dialetical Field." He proposed a major principle of communication theory as practical metadiscourse. This principle acknowledges the reflexivity of communication theory with social practice, and points to our consequent obligations as theorists to address issues in the everyday world of social practices.

Both Cronen (1995a) and Craig (1999) pointed to the role of theory in communicative practice, and as a communicative practice. Most important for me, Cronen addressed directly how to judge the worth of a practical theory—in terms of its social consequences. You may recall that I finished the last chapter with a series of questions, among which were: "What can it mean to take communicating as the focus of our concern? How does it allow us to develop and defend a vision of a just and good society?" In developing the arguments here and treating communicating as the focus of concern, I have arrived at the point where I am now saying that we need to develop a practical theory of communicating, one that is directly assessable in terms of its contribution to a vision of a just and good society.

Such a practical theory will maintain a direct and opening relationship with our practices—one that allows us to go on. It is "a matter of knowing how to move in the patterns of communication in which we live, of finding our way about and of acting wisely" (Pearce, 1994a, p. 7). There is no role for grand theory in acting wisely, but there is a role for coherent, and perhaps liberating, accounts of our practices that can help us proceed. That is the ongoing task of this book.

⟪⟫ Communicating

You may perhaps have noticed that I have increasingly been been using the word *communicating* and not the word *communication*. This may have been jarring or awkward when you first read it. I know I found it so when I started to use the "ing" form rather than the "ion". The jarring or awkwardness once again indicates the entrenchment of a particular way of talking about communication (and not communicating) that I am trying to make visible.

Grammatically, I am making a distinction between the present participle of the verb "to communicate", used either in the present continuous tense or as a gerund, and the static noun form of "communication". In using this present participle, in whatever form, I am emphasising the ongoing temporal aspects of the process. In contrast, the word *communication* is typically used to describe a static entity. Other authors have made an equivalent distinction, although some have glossed over the finer grammatical distinctions and simply distinguished the two forms as verb and noun, respectively

Barnett Pearce (1996) has eloquently captured the difference between these different ways and the need to emphasise the verb rather than the noun form. As he pointed out, the most common expression is *communication* in noun form. When the noun form is used, we are usually taking about such things as persuasion, education, transfer of information, and the like. These are forms of communication in which the outcomes are prefigured and the process is not. The outcome, or at least what could be desirable, is presumed to be already known in the naming (e.g., to educate, to persuade, to transfer information).

In contrast, the verb form of *communicating* focuses on the process, and the outcome is not prefigured. This can be illustrated by such descriptors as dialogue and deliberation. We do not know the outcome of such communicating forms, but can talk about the form of the form, as it were. For example, we can talk about deliberating as the process of comparing your own understanding with that of others, and weighing up the various options and choices. There is no particular outcome prefigured here, only a way of proceeding.

Other communication scholars have noted this difference between noun and verb forms as a difference between products of communication and the process. For example, Sigman (1992, 1995)—in talking about the consequentiality of communication that I introduced in chapter 1—argued that we have a critical choice about communication. We can assume that the important "stuff" goes on behind the scene of the communicative behavior being displayed (in our heads, in our culture, etc). Alternatively, we can assume that the process of communicating itself is significant, or consequential, to human affairs. Sigman made the second choice and went on to argue that the nature of the consequentiality should/might be the appropriate focus for a discipline of communication.

Brenda Dervin (1993) deliberated similarly when she considered the status of the academic field of communication. She saw communication scholarship as focused primarily on entities and not processes; on nouns and not verbs. Yet she went on to argue that the only possibility for a disciplinary status for the field rests in our understanding of the process, not the entity. For such a status to develop, we need to be able to face "the sternest test of all—what happens in the elusive moments of human communicating" (Dervin, 1993, p. 53).

Although Brenda Dervin and Stuart Sigman used the distinction between entity (noun) and process (verb) to point to the requirements for a disciplinary status in the field of communication, the consequences of focusing on the verb (or present participle) form go beyond that. Barnett Pearce's (1996) major contention was that most societies (at least the Western ones with which we are familiar) have chosen to institutionalize the noun form of *communication* and that this very institutionalization is creating the forces that are pulling communities apart. I hinted at this in chapter 2 when I described the consequences of a Lockean view of communication (entity/noun form) for notions of community. This Lockean view actually does not allow any notion of community to come to the fore; rather, it is the individuals and their ideas that predominate.

So, by prefiguring the process of communication in the present continuous form of *communicating*, we are helping to bring notions of community and the social world we inhabit to the fore. This proposition sits well with the arguments of Dewey and the pragmatic philosophers who followed him. For Dewey (1981), it was critical that we take human experience seriously and to do this we needed to value what was in process, not what was presumed finished or ended. As a way of forcing this issue, Dewey also switched from nouns to verbs and gerunds. He showed what happens, for example, when we stop talking about identity and start talking about identifying (Cronen, 1995a). When we do this, we turn to process and relating, and experiencing and changing. Similarly I am trying to show what happens when we stop talking about communication and start talking about communicating.

In making this grammatical shift from nouns to verbs and gerunds, I have also shifted to a new language game in the Wittgensteinian sense. This is a first step in evolving a new grammar, or way of talking, about communicating practices that is a feature of practical theory (Cronen, 1995a). In the ensuing chapters, further grammatical features are added and new ways of talking developed.

4

Understanding where we are—
in communicating

In the first chapter, I said that we need to make a discontinuous leap from where the field of communication is today if it is to get somewhere else in the future—indeed, if it is to get anywhere at all. This leap requires us to treat communicating as the focus of concern; to inquire into communicating and not communication; and to recognize that we construct our reality in communicating. I discussed the first two issues in chapters 2 and 3. Here I am concerned with what it can mean to treat seriously the notion of "constructing our reality in communicating."

When we do start to talk about communicating, we are led into quite a different realm, one where persons in conversation (Harré, 1983), as situated interpreters (Stewart, 1995), are sovereign. As such, there are very fluid boundaries for this realm; they exist and change with our capacity to coconstruct what they are. However, it is not a realm of anarchy that would arise from an extreme relativist's position. It is still orderly, albeit of a different order than conventionally sought. Here, order is to be seen in relationships, not singularities; in happenings, not things; in processes, not outcomes; and in the lived experience of human beings, not their inferred mental processes.

Understanding this realm becomes quite critical when we also realize that as scholars of communicating, we are generating our understanding of communicating in the very same process. What can it mean to us as inquirers into this process of which we are a part? How can we, as Pearce (1994a) put it, find our way around and do so wisely?

In this chapter, I want to explore a notion of participatory knowing and its relationship with the lived experience of communicating. This is an exploration of what it means, to use Heidegger's term, to be a *situated interpreter* (Stewart, 1995)—to engage in sense-making in our relation with others. This exploration leads us to a very different position than that conventionally held in mainstream communication theory and research: Not only does this exploration overturn our conventional understandings of objective knowledge and truth, it also leads us to a reconsideration of notions of morality and aesthetics. This chapter, perhaps more than others, deserves Vern Cronen's warning when he was talking about future directions for social approaches to communication: this is truly "work that is not for the timid" (Cronen, 1995a, p. 224).

ᘑ Knowing and experiencing

A practical way of knowing

Asking questions about different ways of knowing is to ask questions about what it is we know and how we generate this knowledge. Many philosophers and social theorists of this century have drawn on a set of distinctions from Aristotle in the *Nicomachean Ethics* to answer these questions. Essentially, there is a three-fold distinction and I rely on Sensat's (1979) succinct account to describe it.

First, Aristotle drew a line between scientific knowledge and calculative. Then he drew a second set of distinctions from the calculative component to refer to productive (poesis) knowledge and practical (praxis) knowledge. Scientific knowledge is concerned with the generation of universal and necessary truths, making deductions from first principles. Productive, or technical knowledge is concerned with making things, applying art or skill. Practical knowledge, on the other hand, is concerned with doing things—with prudential (phronesis) action oriented to the action itself not to its ends.

Many contemporary philosophers have not only drawn on this distinction but have also noted a neglect or negation of the third, practical form of knowledge. Yet, as Sensat (1979) wrote, understanding practical knowledge is essential, because the capacity to deal rationally with technical or scientific problems is different in kind from that needed to deal with practical problems. This is the same point made by Scott (1998) that I discussed in chapter 1. We need to understand this capacity to deal with practical problems because these are the problems of the human social realm, of communicating. They are also the problems of a practical theory of communicating. To elaborate, I consider the arguments of two authors—Hans-Georg Gadamer and John Shotter—drawing on different, but interestingly compatible, traditions.

Gadamer's (1992) major philosophical concern was with elucidating the hermeneutical nature of the human sciences and human experience generally. He argued against a scientific, pure knowledge approach and for the use of practical knowledge when it comes to understanding the human, social realm. From his hermeneutical stance, the pursuit of pure or scientific knowledge is incompatible with understanding in the social realm. In pursuing pure knowledge, the interpreter is alienated from the interpreted in order to arrive at an objective view. Scientific knowledge is unchangeable and invariable. This is the knowledge I talked about in chapter 2 that was sought by the Enlightenment scholars of the 17th century and by all those who followed in the rationalist/empiricist tradition. However, this form of knowledge is not relevant, indeed not possible, when we come to human beings understanding human beings. Instead, Gadamer wrote that we need to be concerned with practical, or moral, knowledge: "Moral knowledge, as Aristotle describes it, is clearly not objective knowledge—i.e., the knower is not standing over against a situation that he merely observes; he is directly confronted with what he sees. It is something that he has to do" (Gadamer, 1992, p. 314).

This type of moral knowledge, described by Gadamer, has three important features. First, moral knowledge comes out of practice, from human activity itself: It is not something that is rationally discussed and derived. For Gadamer, moral knowledge is in the domain of the full human experience, not separate from it. Although Gadamer did not use the word directly, he was clearly talking about the knowledge that comes out of communicating. Second, moral knowledge is knowledge of particulars that help to direct action in good ways, not to desirable ends. It is knowledge that emerges from particular practices in particular contexts to guide action in that particular situation. This is very different from knowledge that reflects necessary and universal truths. With this claim, Gadamer returned to the position of the casuists that the Enlightenment scholars disparaged so many centuries ago. He also returned to the procedures recommended by Aristotle in the *Nichomachean Ethics*: "Sound moral judgment always respects the circumstances of specific kinds of cases" (Toulmin, 1990, p. 32). Third, moral knowledge is never knowable in advance, as is knowledge that can be taught. We do not possess moral knowledge in such a way that we already have it and then apply it to specific situations; rather, it is in doing things that we bring about our moral knowing. For Gadamer, the conventional, contemporary concept of ethics does not reflect moral knowledge. A list of general ethical injunctions that are expected to be applicable across all situations does not reflect a moral knowing; moral knowledge is always emergent in practice.

Whereas Gadamer's argument relies on Aristotle's major distinction between theoretical knowledge and moral knowledge, Shotter (e.g., 1990, 1993) started with Ryle's (1963) distinction between "knowing that" and "knowing how." "Knowing that" is knowing that something is the case, knowing a fact (e.g., the sun will rise tomorrow); whereas "knowing how" is knowing how to do something by applying rules or criteria (e.g., making bread). Shotter then added a third kind of knowing that he calls "knowing from" (1990, p. 12). This knowing of the third kind is a form of practical knowledge, as Aristotle and later Gadamer characterised it. But Shotter, drawing on Vico, Vygotsky and Mead, emphasized the social realm of this knowing; it is knowing that comes from our relations with others. To quote from Shotter:

> [I]t is knowledge of a moral kind, for it depends upon the judgments of others as to whether it expression or its use is ethically proper or not—one cannot just have it or express it on one's own, or wholly within oneself. It is the kind of knowledge one has only from within a social situation . . . and which thus takes into account (and is accountable to) the others in the social situation. (Shotter, 1993, p. 7)

Shotter made the same point as Gadamer—that moral knowledge is about doing. However, Shotter expanded on this by arguing that moral knowledge is about doing with other people. Moral knowing does not exist independently of a social situation, instead it is brought about within it. You cannot reiterate a long list of professional ethics for this form of "knowing from"—it emerges from what you do. Indeed, for Shotter (1997a), the ethics is there in the joint action before anything else and certainly before any formulation of it: It is prior to and not a consequence of our knowledge. By way of example, Shotter described the feeling of obligation we have to others once we acknowledge their presence: "And it is only from within this obligation that we can . . . fully experience . . . reality through the ethical relations established in our initial acknowledgments" (1997a, p. 7).

Pearce (1994b) similarly observed that when we are involved in the process of communicating our primary question is a moral one—one of "what *should* I do?" The very process of acting in communicating calls forth a series of moral orders of rights, duties, responsibilities, and so on, that starts with the simple process of looking at someone. We all know that feeling of obligation that arises from making eye contact—the obligation to then start talking. That same sense of obligation continues throughout a conversation. This observation about moral obligation is very important, and I return to it later in this chapter.

Here, however, the important point that both Gadamer and Shotter made is that moral knowing is not something we know independent of ourselves or our social living. It is not something that can be learned as a set of ethical rules; rather, we act into and out of our morality. Most important, these authors argued that morality is inherent in practice; it is inherent in our practice of communicating. So it is this practical, moral way of knowing with which we as participator, and inquirers in communicating are concerned. We are concerned with a way of knowing that comes out of what we do in communicating.

Practice and experience

Gadamer and Shotter are among a minority of philosophers who have not dismissed the issue of morality as trivial, or of limited metaphysical curiosity. Instead, in their own ways, they both returned to the classic question of "Does it [morality] reside in the very modality of human existence?" (Bauman, 1991, p. 138). For both of these scholars, the answer is "Yes." John Dewey would also answer "Yes" to the classic question, and Dewey's (1981) reflections help us further in our explorations of participatory knowing.

One of Dewey's lifelong concerns was to affirm the relevance of the commonplace to the most profound philosophical speculation. For him, the most commonplace was everyday experience. He strove to redress the balance against the Cartesian School who relegated experience to a secondary and almost irrelevant place in the scheme of things. This is how Dewey saw the problem:

> The history of the development of the physical sciences is the story of the enlarging possession by mankind of more efficacious instrumental-ities dealing with the conditions of life and action. But when one neglects the connection of these scientific objects with the affairs of primary experience . . . the world is indifferent to human interests because it is apart from experience. (Dewey, 1981, p. 258)

Dewey saw his task as redressing this imbalance, by "creating and promot-ing a respect for human experience and its potentialities" (1981, p. 249). For Dewey, experiences are the things that come about as we act into our world. It is not what we think or feel about it retrospectively, but what happens in the doings of our living—hence his emphasis on the lived experience. Dewey's arguments about experience have a twofold importance for me.

First, they return us to the very practical everyday realm of acting in communicating, of participating in our life. Dewey gave good reason for being concerned with the mundane and the ordinary, with the minutiae of our everyday experiences. He urged us to ask "What do we experience about things we do and happenings in our world?" It is this point of experience that is our empirical reality and the foundation for his philosophic method. It is perhaps important to emphasise there that Dewey's use of the term *exper-ience* is very different and much richer than that of the behaviorists, who also relied on the concept of an empirical reality. For them, experience was no more than a behavioral reaction to events in the world. For Dewey, experience was something else entirely:

> "Experience" denotes the planted fields, the sowed seeds, the reaped harvests, the changes of night and day, spring and autumn . . . that are observed, feared, longed for; it also denotes the the one who plants or reaps, who works or rejoices, hopes, fears, plans . . . It is 'double-barrelled' in that it recognizes in its primary integrity no division between act and material, subject and object, but contains them both in an unanalyzed totality. (Dewey, 1981, p .257)

Second, it is in our lived experiences with others that our practical, moral knowing emerges. If we are to be concerned with a practical way of knowing, we need to return to the ordinary, everyday world of our experiences with others. This is the heart of our inquiry. Indeed, Cronen (1995b) argued for the critical need to recapture this Deweyian concept of experience if we are to proceed with any serious exploration of the phenomenon of communicating. We cannot even attempt to understand what it is to participate—to act with others—if we do not return to our experiences of it. According to Cronen, to return to experience we must cast down "four idols of social research": the idols of the mental theatre, redundancy, beliefs, and hidden mechanisms (Cronen, 1995b, p. 28).

I made reference to the pervasiveness of the "idol of the mental theatre" at the beginning of chapter 3, when I commented that the sense of our bodies as container, for minds, thoughts, and the like is such a dominant root metaphor in the English language that it is hard to conceive otherwise. From the point of view of social science, which posits cognitive, affective and conative constructs in the mind, the real challenge has been to understand how these operate a priori to experience. However, as Cronen noted "The research that has resulted has been a welter of findings that tax the interpretative abilities of even the most clever researchers" (Cronen, 1995b, p. 28).

The idol of redundancy finds its home in the search for statistical or quantitative regularities in conversational patterns. The argument, well advocated by Cappella (1990), holds that the most useful way to understand human action is in terms of the patterns of redundancy against a background of randomness. But, as Cronen (1995b) argued, we as practitioners know that regularity is no sign of enriching interaction and that a single one-off event may be more profound in terms of understanding than regular actions, especially those that are quantifiable. The key point here is that the experiences of communicating cannot be reduced to aggregate data expressed quantitatively. I return to this issue in more depth in chapter 7 where I discuss research practices.

According to Cronen (1995b), the idol of beliefs arises not because beliefs are necessarily irrelevant to experience, but instead because they are treated as independent propositions or bits of knowledge. As such, beliefs are seen as separate from and prior to our experiences in communicating. Yet, if we are take the story being developed here seriously, it is clear we must deny this idol and assert that beliefs arise in experience and contribute to it.

Finally, there is the idol of hidden mechanisms: mechanisms that we cannot see, touch, hear or smell, but that must be there to account for our experiences and actions. There must be something behind the appearance of things, or why else would we do what we do? For me, the positing of the hidden mechanism of attitude is typical of this idolization. Because psychologists observed people acting in certain consistent ways, they proposed the hidden mechanism of attitude to account for it. We do this, or don't do this, because we have a positive attitude or a negative attitude to it. Again, this obscures the more obvious place to look for our understandings of why things happen the way they do—in communicating.

All of these idols, or notions, presume that the things that go on inside our heads are the important things for which we have to account. They presume that what we do in the world is driven by these hidden mechanism inside our head. They also presume that all these things come before communicating. This is, in essence, a cognitive approach to explanation. It assumes the intramental plane of existence that I discussed and eschewed in chapter 3.

A cognitive approach can only construe communication in the entity/ noun form. Indeed, for cognitivists, communication is not a focus at all; rather, it is the individuals who behave in certain ways because of the hidden mechanisms in their mind. However, when you contemplate this form of explanation, it becomes quite bizarre. As Harré (1983), among others (e.g., Cronen, 1995b; Shotter, 1984), noted, the conclusion far more parsimonious with the data is that our abilities are "primarily public and collective, located in talk" (Harré, 1983, p. 21). We can directly see and hear our actions in talk. That is the primary data, without any need to infer a hidden mechanism in our minds.

So, once we step away from any cognitive approach to explanation, we can return to experience. Experience leads us directly to embodied persons in the real world (Cronen, 1995b)—to us, as people, communicating. As scholars of communicating, we are also embodied persons in the real world, and it is our lived experience in communicating that is the fount of our practical knowledge.

✍ Finding our way about

I have described a picture of communicating as a process in which we generate our knowing from within the very process itself. This is a "knowing from" that comes out of our lived experiences with others, and is the core of our concern here. This is, as Harré (1983) argued, the primary human reality: persons in conversations.

But how do we find our way around in this process and, more important, how can we do it wisely? Let's talk about the problem as a navigational one, and imagine sailors in some distant sea. How do they get around, and how do they do it wisely? The essence of it is both movement forward and periodic way-checking. The sailors take their measurements, identify where they are and set the course, changing sails or moving around for wind, and so on. Things happen during the course and a rechecking is needed. Then they go on again. Note that within this metaphor navigation is never complete, you never stay in the one position, so you have to keep taking fixes (or dead reckonings).

When we are in communicating, we are not alone, but we still proceed in a manner similar to that of the sailor: We move on doing things and we make periodic reassessments. Moving on and assessing, however, have certain fundamental differences as they are done from different positions, with different consequences.

Knowing our position

When we are moving on in communicating, we are engaged in the practical, moral knowing that I talked about earlier. However, to assess where we are, we have to step away from the actual doing—the participating—if only for the moment. Once we are outside the process we make a different type of assessment, a different type of judgment, from a different position. For Dewey (1981), making judgments outside the process is akin to the aesthetic experience, not the moral. Judgments made outside the process have an aesthetic quality because they round out an experience into completeness and unity—they provide a momentary understanding of the pattern, structure, and coherence of an experience.

As with the notion of moral experience, introduced earlier in this chapter, the idea of the aesthetic experience being used here is much broader than that relegated to the world of art. Indeed, Dewey (1934) wrote at length on the importance of seeing the aesthetic in a broader, more everyday way; to point to our human capacity to grasp a sense of order, of harmony, out of our experiences. For Dewey, there was a continuity in our aesthetic experiences and the normal processes of living. However, this aesthetic judgement can only be made, to use Dewey's words, from the "consumer's" standpoint, not the "producers." When we are talking about communicating, an aesthetic judgment can only be made—however momentarily—outside of the process of participating ("producing").

Thus, what I am suggesting here are two different positions that allow two different types of experience in a moral and an aesthetic domain, respectively. In many significant ways, this parallels the arguments of Bakhtin (1990; Morson & Emerson,1989). According to Bakhtin, all text or lived experience contains a hero (sometimes present and sometimes implied) and ethics/morality belongs to the hero and her or his actions. On the other hand, aesthetics belongs to the author or beholder of the hero and her or his actions. We find ourselves in this authorial role whenever we want to understand, to make sense of our experience of participating. In this authorial role we are brought into a narrative frame out of a direct participating one. We make our judgments in this narrative frame and the judgments are aesthetic ones. We act to provide coherence and a sense of harmony to the experience that we have participated in.

Yet, while understanding, or generating the narrative, is done in the aesthetic mode, it still has moral import (Bakhtin, 1990). The moral import lies in the nature of the narrative generated, the values expressed, and the way in which it allows us to move on (or not, as the case may be). As participants, we can take these narratives, or momentary understandings, back to the participating process. They are, in fact, our offerings to the mutual process for consideration. The moral import is experienced in these offerings in the process. As an example, consider a conversation in which two people are talking about their relationship. At some point, one of the people says, "Oh, there you go again, you just aren't listening!" In saying this, the person has momentarily stepped out of the moral domain of participation, made an aesthetic judgment, and offered it back in the process of participating. The particular moral import of this judgment is evidenced by the ensuing actions of the participants, which I am sure I can leave to your imagination.

We do this sort of thing continually in our conversations; indeed, so continually that, in practice, we couldn't draw the line between the two domains. Nevertheless, the distinction between the aesthetic and the moral further adds to the new language game being developed here. In particular, by drawing on Dewey and Bakhtin, I have introduced the aesthetic into the act of living, of communicating. Further, I have argued that morality and aesthetics are intertwined. Whether we are making moral or aesthetic judgments depends on our positions, and the two types of positions are interdependent. The judgments we make outside are in the aesthetic dimension; the work we do inside is moral work.

Moving between

It is important to remember that even though I have made a distinction between the role of hero in the moral dimension and the role of author in the aesthetic dimension, these are only useful fictions, as it were. Nothing is stationary in communicating—we are always moving on and moving between. So what is it we are doing when we are moving between? I want to suggest that this moving between could usefully be thought of as a "trueing" process. Again, I am drawing on Dewey for my arguments here. Recall that at the end of chapter 2, I mentioned Dewey's arguments about the need to move from the entity/noun form to the gerund/verb form. Well, he has argued similarly for the notion of truth.

McDermott, who edited the *Philosophy of John Dewey*, described Dewey's arguments in his essay on "The Experimental Theory of Knowledge" as follows:

> Dewey stresses the "intending" character of knowing and the relational character of truth. Dewey writes that "fulfilment, completion are always relative terms. Hence the criterion of the truth or falsity of the meaning . . . lies within the relationships of the situation and not without." He prefers the adverb "truly" to the abstract noun "truth", but perhaps it can be said that what he points to are our attempts at "trueing." (McDermott in Dewey, 1981, pp. 175–6)

I find this concept of trueing useful in three ways. First, it directs our attention to process rather than any static, invariant quality: Trueing is an action we engage in with others, not a thing to be found or proved. This reflects Rorty's (1989) argument about the contingency of language: Truth is created in our talk. But here, rather than imply that a thing is created, I want to suggest that things are pointed to in our talk.

Second, Dewey's notion of trueing directs our attention to relational features rather than abstract qualities: Our attempts at trueing are interdependent with the context, not apart from it. Here, we can refer back to the very start of chapter 2, where I talked about context in a complex sense, as existing in a reflexive relationship with the text. In this more complex sense, meaning is generated from the mutual interplay of context and utterance. Similarly, our attempts at trueing occur in this same interplay.

Third, Dewey's notion of trueing directs our attention to local rather than universal features: Trueing occurs in specific contexts and its value lies within the local relationships at work, not any universal ones. This, of course, returns us to a way of thinking that predates the Enlightenment moves described in chapter 2. Most important, it reopens the possibility for the application of sound moral judgement of the kind referred to by Aristotle.

This notion of trueing is clearly interdependent with the other two notions of morality and aesthetics which I introduced earlier. Indeed, the three concepts are inseparable. As we are moving on in the moral domain of experiencing, we periodically make navigational checks in the aesthetic realm, and it is in bringing our checks back into experiencing that we could be said to be trueing. I appreciate that this proposition can be hard to grasp—it certainly has been for me. It might help if I turn to another way of looking at the issues before we return to what it means in practice, in our communicating.

⟐ Reconstruing the classic questions

What I've written so far is actually a radical reconstruction of some perennial, classic questions concerning notions of truth, goodness, and beauty. This reconstruing has come about both because I have orientated to the process of communicating and not to the entity/noun form, and because of the move back into our lived experiences in the human realm of communicating. In other words, it has occurred through the discontinuous leap we are making; a leap that takes us into a world where communicating is material and does matter.

With the leap made here, I have not only reconstrued all three notions but have also brought two back into the fore—those of morality and aesthetics. It seems to me that over the last 3 centuries of modernity, we have witnessed a relegation of the notions of morality and aesthetics to the backseat, while scholars have relentlessly pursued their search for abstract, invariant, and universal truths.

In this section, I want to quickly sketch a picture of how notions of morality, aesthetics, and truth have been conventionally taken and then, by way of contrast, draw out how I am using these notions here. My brief picture makes no attempt at being an encyclopedic tour of these three perennial questions— that would be a book in itself. Nor am I even pretending to evaluate, critically or otherwise, different approaches. Instead, my aim is simply to sketch a primitive overview to act as the backdrop for apprehending another way.

Understandings of morality and aesthetics

In his account of classical Greek thinking, Bernstein (1992) eloquently argued that the scope of what the Greeks took to be the proper ethical-political domain is far broader and richer than modern understandings of morality. Conventional, modern understandings of morality are, in fact, quite impoverished and limited in scope. This conventional understanding is characterized by four main features.

First, the concept of morality is relegated to an extraordinarily narrow domain and, most typically, the domain of the religious. Consider, for example, the teaching of morality in schools. Where, if at all, is it explicitly taught? It is addressed in classes on religion. Indeed, I have frequently experienced this direct equating of morality with religion when I have spoken on this topic. Scholars and laypersons alike have typically taken my use of the word moral to reflect a religious, compared with, for example, a scientific view.

Second, in mainstream philosophy morality lies in the realm of reasoned principle (Harré, 1983). Morality is something that must be rationally discussed and derived. It is a set of principles objectively established and, thus, independent of human beings and their social context. This is one of the Enlightenment turns that I described in chapter 2, drawing on the work of Toulmin (1990), and that I referred to in the previous section in reference to Dewey's notion of trueing.

Third, the concept of morality has been instrumentalized as "ethics." I deliberately use quotation marks here because the concept of ethics as taught in most professional degrees these days is far from the concept of ethics as proposed by Aristotle. Today, ethics is typically taken as a set of injunctions or guiding principles for professional behavior, inevitably context free and timeless. To quote a colleague caricaturizing the position of others, ethics is "a set of sentences that describe moral imperatives that we follow when convenient and cite as excuses for doing dastardly things" (Pearce, 1994a, p. 10).

Fourth, our modern conventional understanding of morality is that it is unimportant. Bauman (1991), in a fascinating account of the social manipulation of morality, argued that questions of morality are dismissed as of no more than purely academic interest and then usually as some mere metaphysical curiosity. Writing from a sociological perspective, Bauman argued that the very discipline has no language to deal with issues of morality. "And what one cannot speak of is bound to remain silent" (Bauman, 1991, p. 138). The same could be said of all our modern human/social disciplines, including communication studies.

It is interesting to look a little more closely at Bauman's (1991) account. He maintained that social organization is able to neutralize the impact of moral action through three complementary arrangements. What is fascinating about these three arrangements is that they have direct implications for communication and what we take it to be.

In the first arrangement, the distance between action and its consequences is stretched so far that the actors cannot comprehend the consequences of their acts. It is only the task and the procedural, technical rules that count to guide action, not the moral import. Let's resay this by considering the classic transmission model of communication, in which you have a sender, channel with a message, and a receiver. In that model, participants in the communication process are kept apart by the channel and the message. Theories based on this conception are concerned with how the sender can manipulate the message for the sender's reasons. The integral relation between sender and receiver is ignored, because the medium keeps them separate, and thus any moral import of action is trivialized.

Second, those who may feel the moral import of another's actions are kept away from the presence of the other, or denied any encountering space. Communications technology has been used to great effect in this regard. We now have a plethora of hardware and software that can guarantee you never have to see a human face that "might become visible and glare as a moral demand" (Bauman, 1991, p. 145). For Bauman, and myself, the physical presence of the other in conversation is essential to experiencing moral import. I talked about this earlier in the discussion on a practical way of knowing. There, I said that once we acknowledge the presence of another, by something as simple as eye contact, a whole sway of moral obligations are established.

Third, those who may feel the moral import of the other's action are dissembled; they are turned from human beings into a collection of different attributes or traits in aggregate form. Thus, the moral import falls on no person at all. Consider the role of public opinion polling in this regard. What individual people believe about the moral import of, say, a government's action, is dissembled into percentages of belief statements cross-tabulated with different socioeconomic status or age groups. Where are the people in this? Where is the construction of a mutual understanding or recognition of mutual consequences? The answer is nowhere.

So why is it that the narrower, instrumental view of morality—the view that relegates moral issues to an unimportant position in our way of living— the one that holds? Why is it that communication scholars have, in the main, neglected issues of morality? The answer to these questions is the same. Our society has a narrow, unimportant view of morality, and communication scholars have neglected moral issues, because of the Enlightenment heritage I described in chapter 2. We lost the broad notion of morality that Bernstein (1992) referred to as classical when the Enlightenment project tried to justify moral principles objectively (Gadamer, 1992; Macintyre, 1985). At the same time, we lost the broad and rich notion of what it could mean to communicate when Enlightenment scholars redefined communication as trivial.

Our conventional modern understanding of aesthetics is as limited as that of morality, and for much the same reasons. First, the concept of aesthetics has been primarily confined to the world of art, design, and literature in much the same way that morality has been centralized in religion. In other words, the aesthetic experience is seen to be specific to a certain rarefied arena of creation. Although it has been the focus of extensive debate in that arena, it is not generally discussed outside of it.

Second, aesthetics has been confined to a narrow abstract and analytic domain in mainstream philosophy during the past century (Shusterman, 1992). Gadamer (1992) also was critical of our modern understanding of a work of art and our experience of it. As he saw it, that understanding depended on a process of abstraction: "By disregarding everything in which a work is rooted . . . , it becomes visible as 'the pure work of art' " (Gadamer, 1992, p. 85). Once again, we have a depiction of aesthetics as independent of humans and the social context of their experience.

Third, the aesthetic dimension has been dismissed, or demeaned, from the concern of communication scholars. Indeed, in the area of popular culture and cultural studies—where we could perhaps most expect some concern with the aesthetic—it has been classed as "really useless knowledge" (Bennett, 1987). Even when cultural values are raised, "aesthetic issues . . . are subordinated to the necessities of ideological interpretation" (Frith, 1991, p. 105). In other words, the aesthetic realm is of secondary interest, if any at all, to that of politics and related issues.

Given the limited mainstream approach to aesthetics, it is no wonder the notion has been dismissed. Given also the neglect of the lived experience, it is no wonder that aesthetics is seen to have little importance. However, Shusterman (1992) strongly recommended Dewey's (1934) down-to-earth philosophy of the aesthetic as a real antidote to the mainstream approach. As we discussed earlier, when we return the notion of the aesthetic to the broader domain of the lived experience, we have a different notion indeed. In that broader domain, aesthetic considerations become everyday. They are considerations that we all engage in when apprehending a sense of closure, of completeness, in our experiences, however temporarily.

Dewey (1934) was not only the philosopher to call for a return of the aesthetic to the broader domain of the full human experience. Gadamer (1992) also argued extensively for the need to view the experience of art in such a way that it be understood as just that—experience. In returning the aesthetic to the realm of experience, we are, according to Gadamer, returning it to being a hermeneutical phenomenon: one that raises questions of our understanding in the historical context of our living. For Gadamer, our experience of the aesthetic is a mode of understanding. So here, I take this broader notion of the aesthetic experience because of its compatibility with the need to develop ways of understanding the complex and challenging process of communicating.

Understandings of truth

Truth is a concept with which all scholars are familiar. It is what typically preoccupies them in their research (Is it true? How can we prove it is true?) and in their philosophical writings (What is truth?). In most instances, this questioning and reasoning is premised, in some way or another, on the fundamental assumptions that brought about the Enlightenment.

However, the realm in which we are moving cannot accommodate the commonsense or correspondence notion of truth: that a statement is true if it conforms with the facts or agrees with reality. In the realm here, there is no independent reality with which to agree. Our realm also cannot accommodate those other theories of truth, such as coherence theory, that treat truth as a timeless and unchanging thing, unaffected by the particularities of the context. Indeed, according to Campbell: "Whether we can work out a different conception of truth, or whether we have to give up on truth altogether seems to me to be one of the profound philosophical challenges of our time" (Campbell, 1992, p. 6).

In earlier writings (e.g., Penman, 1992), I quoted Francis Bacon as my response to this challenge raised by Campbell: "What is truth? said jesting Pilate; and would not stay for an answer" (Speake, 1979, p. 355). Here and now I can no longer be so completely dismissive, because Campbell's compelling argument on truth and historicity has offered me a way forward. I draw on his argument here with gratitude.

Campbell began his argument by recognising there is much in ordinary experience that casts doubts on the usefulness of the concept of truth, not the least of which is the recognition of what he calls *historicity*—"that through our actions we constitute who we are" (Campbell, 1992, p. 1). It is clear that Campbell's notion of historicity bears much in common with the form of constructionism assumed here. He proceeded to propose that instead of taking the conventional notion of truth (as dialectically opposed to historicity) we locate the notion of truth firmly in action, particularly in linguistic practice. This is not dissimilar to Rorty's (1989) notion of the contingency of language that I mentioned earlier. However, Campbell developed his argument in such a way as to help round out my story construction process. By a series of rigorously developed steps, Campbell leads us in an exploration of what it can mean to locate truth firmly in action. For me, he makes a number of critical points.

First, he turned the abstract notion of truth into an adverb, and wrote about "acting truly"—an echo of Dewey. "[I]f we are to act truly, our approach to entities in the world must maintain an open attitude, so that we let them show themselves as they are" (Campbell, 1992, p. 425). There is a twofold openness required: We need to be open in our pointing to how things are in talk and things need to be revealing something of how they are. When we turn to communicating, acting truly calls for a reciprocal openness between participants, allowing things to be revealing. This is not an easy task. All too often in everyday communicating, we have a tendency to quickly impose interpretations, to make decisions about what is going on or what was said. To remain open requires us to hold off our too-quick interpretations and to allow for other possibilities to emerge.

Second, Campbell (1992) argued that the notion of understanding is far more appropriate than the notion of knowledge. Our use of the word *knowledge* is too closely linked with an on/off, or real/false, notion: that is, we do know or we don't know, and what we know is either true or it is false. When we are searching for knowledge, we are more prone to the too-quick interpretation mentioned above. In contrast, the word *understanding* lends itself far more to a sense of degree. Our understanding can be partial or incomplete but nevertheless there, in some way or another. Our understanding also acknowledges the possibility that we could have more of it. Even when you say you understand that something is the case, this does not stop you from understanding that case better. When we are striving for understanding (cf. knowledge), we do not deny that there could be more of the entity to appear. Seeking understanding is more likely to keep us open.

Third, in acting truly toward understanding, we are at the same time committed to the continual possibility of revision in the light of a more adequate apprehension. This acknowledges the very temporal and context-bound nature of all communicating, and provides for the transitory nature of what we understand. Truth is not an uncompromisable, universal fact; rather, it is a contextually bound local phenomenon. However, as Campbell (1992) pointed out, recognizing the socially constructed and therefore changeable nature of our search for understanding is no justification for regarding questions of truth as irrelevant (as I earlier confessed to). As he wrote: "Socially constructed realities may not be timeless or impervious to political action, but they are real nevertheless" (Campbell, 1992, p. 430).

Fourth, Campbell argued "Being true is an achievement attained when the commitments expressed in making the statement, or in performing the deed, are fulfilled" (p. 436). For Campbell, being true is being faithful. Campbell noted that this notion of being true as faithful returns us to a much earlier conception of truth shown in the Old English root of the word, meaning "good faith." Indeed, there was a similar understanding in ancient Greece (before Plato purged it). Truth in the Homeric sense required such things as fidelity, loyalty, constancy, and allegiance. When we apply this notion to communicating, being true is acting faithfully into our social situations. It is acting with integrity and insight towards others and the reality—however socially constructed—of the situation.

To sum up Campbell's argument: "The truth, therefore, is not to be found by renouncing our historicity, nor in trying to construct an impersonal and timeless account of reality which flies in the face of our own humanity. It is rather to be achieved in the quality and authenticity of our faithful life-activities" (Campbell, 1992, p. 438). Campbell very much turned the notion of truth around with his philosophical investigations of another possibility. He transformed it into an activity (a verb) that is ongoing and essentially moral in character, for to evaluate activities as true requires us to ask questions about faithfulness, integrity, authenticity, and the like. This can be nothing else but an ongoing open inquiry in our communicating, an inquiry that can only be undertaken in the practical, moral way of knowing with which I started this chapter.

◖◗ Doing it wisely

With each of the concepts discussed in this chapter, I have taken them from one realm—the abstract, decontextualized world—to another—to the realm of experiencing in communicating. In doing this, I have been developing a different way of talking with different possibilities to help us in our "leap." I am not even trying to suggest that this new realm is how things really are, but merely that this way of talking about it may keep us open enough to be true(ing). What I am offering is a way of making sense of the world of experiencing in communicating in terms of a reworking of the classic questions about goodness, beauty, and truth, couched in a framework of practical knowing. These questions now become ones of what it means to act truly, experience beauty and do good.

In the end, what counts is how this way of talking offers us a way to live as wise human beings. So here I want to hint at (with more to come later) a concept of practical wisdom that somehow integrates the very slippery and interwoven domains of the moral, the aesthetic and the truthful. I have deliberately used the word *wise* here, instead of such words as *logical* or *rational* to emphasize with this way of talking the humanness of the domain we are in. To engage in communicating wisely requires more than mere knowledge; it also calls for experience in doing it and the capacity to do it well. This is the practical knowing I talked about both at the beginning of this chapter and in chapter 1. But now I prefer to drop the word *knowledge* or *knowing* and change the phrase to *practical wisdom*.

For the purposes of our discussion in this chapter, I have made a convenient separation among the aesthetic, moral, and truthful domains, but throughout all domains runs a moral thread. If we return to the Bakhtinian notions of hero and author I discussed earlier, you may recall that although it is the hero's way to act morally and the author's way to act aesthetically, this aesthetic consideration still has moral import. You may also recall that from the discussion of Campbell's (1992) deliberations, that acting truly has a moral force: It is acting in good faith.

So I suggest here that acting truly is doing it wisely; it is the moral order that binds the moral and aesthetic. In acting truly, we are engaging in a particular way of participating in communicating—we are participating in good faith. Also, in acting truly we are engaging in a particular way of making aesthetic judgments—with an open attitude, open to continual revisions. It is in acting truly that we move between the moral and the aesthetic and, in so doing, we bind them in good faith. In chapter 6, I return to how we can do this at a more practical level.

The critical point to be made here is that the moral thread is inescapable; at least in this domain. It is inescapable both in our practice of communicating and in our theorizing and researching in it. Given this, I believe it is essential that we develop ways of talking about it openly and of exploring it in our scholarly practice. This is the theme of the following chapter in which I talk about how we can make moral judgments of, and in, communicating.

5

Judging with moral import,
in good faith

The importance of acting wisely becomes apparent when we consider a further aspect of the problematic nature of communicating—all of our social understandings generated in communicating are based on value. Because our understandings are not independent of ourselves and our communicative actions, all our understandings and actions have a valuational base. In this view there is no such thing as pure description: Every name, every theory, and every account, is based on value. Applying a name, a theory, or an account, brings about a transformation based on value (Sless, 1981).

In the last chapter, I described three fundamental values—those relating to goodness, beauty, and truth—in a new light. In this chapter, I want to explore what these reconstrued values mean for our way of conceiving of communicating and our ways of making judgments about it. As I discussed in chapter 4, when we recover experience and focus on the process of communicating, we need to ask questions of the process that include the moral and aesthetic realms.

What can it mean to say that something is good communicating? How can we make such judgments in good faith? What can it mean when our judgments about communicating come from within the process we are talking about? To address these questions, I draw on the arguments of the previous chapter to develop a way of making judgments (aesthetic domain) about the process, with moral import, while acting in good faith. Substantial parts of the argument are taken from a previous article (Penman, 1992), but they are so important to the development of the current argument I have reproduced them, albeit with some revision.

ᘓ A basis for judging

Outside of the process?

Judgments about communication typically use concepts of effects, or goal achievements or the like. The effects research tradition, especially in mass communication, (e.g., see McQuail, 1987) well illustrates the preoccupation with effects in the communication literature. It would seem that we have a similar preoccupation in our everyday life. In our practical communicative activities, the common descriptions of everyday acts usually rely on some assumption of effect or goal: consider, for example, expressions like "that was attention grabbing" or "that had little impact." But despite the fact that we frequently use these type of judgments in everyday life, they are not without their problems, especially when considered within a broad social construction-ist framework.

In the first instance, although communicative action is judged in terms of the effects it brings about, these types of judgments are not strictly those of communicating per se. Instead, they are judgments about whether communicating brought about what the individual wanted out of the process. They are judgments of individual actions and effects, not of an intersubjective process. They are judgments that assume communication in the entity/noun form.

Second, to be able to make judgments about effects requires the demarcation of an effect from its antecedent (i.e., you must be able to isolate the action from the consequence at a point in time). Yet, even as that effect occurs, the communication process continues and the retrospective and emergent contexts, essential for meaning inference, change. The identification of an effect, then, is based on an essentially arbitrary punctuation of an ongoing interactive process. However, the term *arbitrary*, is not meant to imply capriciousness, randomness, or lack of structure, but to indicate the infinite range of alternatives that are available. There are a multitude of alternative effects that could be demarcated, depending on the points of punctuation, and there are a multitude of alternative interpretations for any one frame. In other words, the identification of effects is as problematic as any other meaning generation process.

Third, there is an important moral issue raised by the use of effects to make judgments about communication. When prime attention is placed on effects, the means by which the effects are brought about—the communicating process—tend to be ignored. Instead, both evaluation and practice are focused on the goal or effect to be achieved, not on the desirability or otherwise of the means. The serious moral implications of this are well demonstrated in Macintyre's (1985) powerful analysis of the moral order in the Western world.

Macintyre (1985) viewed the moral order in the Western world as essentially an amoral one, in which any genuine distinction between manipulative and non-manipulative relations among people has been obliterated. As such, it seems impossible for people to perceive of communication as anything but a manipulative tool. According to Macintyre (1985), we have lost touch with communication-as-narrative—as on-going creation—and simply take it as an instrument for our personal ends. When communication is taken as such, it is impossible to engage in what Macintyre called a "moral quest": Communication cannot be seen as something that allows us to discover or create, when it is only seen as a means to personal ends.

There are strong parallels between Macintyre's (1985) argument and those of Bauman's (1991) which I discussed in the previous chapter. You may recall that Bauman argued that social organization is able to neutralise the impact of moral action through a series of arrangements and that I showed how these arrangements presume an instrumental and/or transmission view of communication. In other words, such a view of communication (note again the need for the noun form) is one that negates or denies the moral implications.

An analysis of the assumptions of the mainstream approaches to communication studies would place most of them in this category of an instrumental view. Here I am referring to the two main traditions or schools identified by Rogers (1982) as empirical (or administrative) and critical. Numerous authors have argued that these two traditions are fundamentally different; in terms both of research practices and their assumptions about communication (e.g., Melody & Mansell, 1983; Smythe & Van Dinh, 1983). When focus is placed on the assumptions of communication, these two traditions are identified as employing either a transmission (empirical) or semiotic (critical/cultural studies) model of communication (e.g., Fiske, 1982). Yet, despite all the claims to differences between them, they share the same base assumptions that lead to communication being seen simply as the instrument to bring about an effect (Penman, 1988). Let me elaborate in terms of three common themes, recognizing that as I do so I am having to treat the two main traditions in rather simple, generalized terms.

First, people are seen as separate from their activities; in particular, the critical activity of meaning generation. From the transmission perspective, meanings are found in the word packages sent to others; they do not emerge out of joint action. From the mainstream semiotic perspective, people are also demarcated from their activities—in this instance the production of texts. People are seen simply as part of the ideological/meaning production system and it is the latter that produces the text, not the people per se. In fact, in many semiotic writings there is a rather strange neglect of people, as active, constituting beings

Second, the relational or interactive nature of the process is ignored or denied. From the transmission perspective, the actions of people are seen to be separate, contiguous behaviors—a message is sent and then received. In the more traditional models from this perspective, there appears to be a presumption of both linear causality and mechanistic behavior. Similarly, from the mainstream semiotic perspective, there is no consideration of the basic relational nature of reading texts. Often it is as if the reading is just there, waiting to be found, rather than generated out of an interaction between the reader and the text.

Third, both approaches treat communication as an instrument for something else. In the transmission view, communication is the instrument by which people produce effects on one another. In the mainstream semiotic view, communication is the instrument by which cultural texts are produced (albeit separate from the people) and ideological struggles engaged. In both approaches there is a failure to treat the process of communicating as a genuine focus of concern. Communication is, as I said in chapter 2, merely the site or topic for something far more interesting.

In contrast, the framework, or language game, I am developing here places its emphasis on the constructive and creative aspects of communicating rather than on the instrumental/manipulative. This constructive framework leads to a preoccupation with the means rather than the ends. As such, the criteria for making judgments need to be concerned with the process itself, not with any arbitrarily identified effects of it.

Or inside?

If you rigorously follow through with a social constructionist argument, it is impossible to base any form of evaluation outside of communicating. Making any evaluation of the process relies on meaning generation that is part of the process itself. It is impossible to get out of communicating to make a judgment of it. The position you take may change—from acting into to generating a narrative/account about—but both positions are still within the process of communicating.

This seeming paradox is analogous to one that arises around the issue of communication and intent. In the past, various theoretical attempts were made to differentiate communication from other behavior in terms of whether the participants intended to communicate (one of those hidden mechanism assumptions I talked about in chapter 4). Although in theory this may appear reasonable, in practice it is not possible to know of an intent without asking about it. In other words, to establish the existence of an intention, the researcher must ask the possible participants about their intention and thus force them to engage in the very same process whose existence they are attempting to establish.

There appear to be inescapable grounds, then, for proposing that the criteria for evaluating communicating cannot be outside of the process. Grounding the criteria for evaluation within the process is the solution taken by a number of recent social theorists, most notably Habermas (e.g., see McCarthy, 1984). Although Habermas' theory of communicative action has been subject to some criticism (e.g., Bernstein, 1983; Burleson & Kline, 1979; Rorty, 1980), we do not have to rely on the criticized assumptions to proceed. For the moment, it suffices to recognize, along with Bernstein (1983), that while Habermas' theory does have problems, his moral-political intentions are still to be lauded. Here, I wish to respect those intentions but develop an alternative argument that does not require the positing of rational criteria.

To do this, it helps to return to a key point in Habermas' claims and one that Bernstein (1983) noted is common to other authors, such as Gadamer, Arendt, and Rorty. These four theorists recognized that the communicative ideals they were positing are somehow already immanent in the communicating community, but not realized in practice. They did not merely state that the ideals are historically situated in existing communities in the sense of traditions; rather, they stated that the very phenomenon of communicating presupposes a certain set of communicative ideals. Rather than positing a set of communicative ideals that are rationally based, as Habermas did, it may perhaps be sufficient to simply ask what is it that there is a possibility of, but not necessarily or always realized in practice. What is it that we cannot/are unable to account for because of our officially accepted ways of talking about communication? To use Shotter's (1987) phrase: What is it in our communicating, and our talk of it, that is currently "rationally invisible" that we could make visible?

At this point it is pertinent to return to one of Campbell's arguments: "If we are to act truly, our approach to entities in the worlds must maintain an open attitude, so that we *let them show themselves as they are*" (1992, p. 425, emphasis added). Thus, to ask what can we make visible that is currently rationally invisible is to ask a question of good faith. By making the rationally invisible visible, we are in fact engaged on a path of acting truly.

In what follows I want to propose a set of communication characteristics that much of contemporary communication theory, and everyday talk about communication, makes rationally invisible. I wish to suggest that these characteristics could well form the basis for an evaluation of communicating. I propose that we use the characteristics of communicating, as seen from within this framework, to judge whether in practice good communicating has occurred or not. In other words, I propose a principle of self-affirmation: Good communicating affirms all the characteristics of itself, it is true to itself. On the other hand, bad communicating renders aspects of the process invisible; it does not reflect good faith with the process of communicating.

Rather than basing the criteria for evaluation on a set of rational characteristics, I propose to explore here the use of its actual characteristics. The concept of "actual characteristics" is, of course, a rather slippery one in the current framework. In a truly "Alice Through the Looking Glass" way, the current framework leads us to the position that what is actual is what we make to be actual. This circularity is unavoidable, but not impossible to work with. In the very building of my story so far, certain characteristics of communicating are implied. Thus, if we accept the story, then we can accept that there are certain actual characteristics of communicating.

This is very much in keeping with Wittgenstein's (1969) proposals about the nature of certainty. For Wittgenstein, certainty was not about absolute truth, but instead about ways of seeing certain things and not others in a given picture of the world. Certainty lies firmly in the realm of values—what it is we value and what we don't in our language game. We become certain about things we value. What I am saying is that within the language game of my story, there are particular characteristics of communicating about which I have little doubt; especially because they are part of the core values of this language game. I am certain that communicating has constituting, contextualizing, diversifying, and open-ended properties. These properties are described next, integrating material from earlier chapters in a different way.

⒧ Evaluating communicating

Constituting

Given that our understanding is socially constituted in communicating, then communicating creates our social world. Communicating has self-generating capacities and these capacities arise out of the very interaction of participants, not out of the properties of their external environment. As Sless (1986) pointed out, there are striking parallels between this self-generating proposition for communicating and propositions of quantum theory. He cited one physicist, trying to come to terms with the counterintuitive (at least counter to an empiricist) world of quantum mechanics, who noted:

> May the universe in some strange sense be 'brought into being' by the participation of those who participate? . . . The vital act is the act of participation. 'Participator' is the incontrovertible new concept given by quantum mechanics. It strikes down the term 'observer' of classical theory . . . . It [observing] cannot be done, quantum mechanics says. (Wheeler, Thorne, & Misner, 1973, p. 1273)

In this vital act of participation, we can find ourselves in a rather different place than traditionally thought: "Rather than acting out of an inner plan or schema, we can think of ourselves as acting 'into' our own present situation" (Shotter, 1986, p. 203). This acting into occurs whenever we engage in communicating, whether it be to make sense of the world of quantum mechanics or to make sense of our personal relationships. Communicating, then, is not only self-generating, it is also self-specifying. It is self-specifying in the sense that our past activities point to the direction of our present ones. This self-specifying aspect of communication has also been described by earlier authors, including Dewey (1981) and Mead (1934). And, as Shotter (1986) demonstrated, the argument can be traced back to Vico writing in the 17th century (the earliest "anti-modern", according to Lilla, 1993).

This constituting characteristic of communicating, both its self-generating and self-specifying aspects, has important ramifications for our concept of meaning. Meaning cannot be anything fixed and invariant; rather, it is constantly changing with our every act of participation. Meaning is a relational phenomenon that is brought about in the interaction of participants. Mead (1938) proposed an analogous argument when he claimed that there are two characteristics that belong to the term *meaning*: that of participation and communicability. Meaning, for Mead, arises out of an act of participation or joint action that, in some aspects at least, creates a sufficiently shared framework for communicability. This parallels Vico's account, as presented by Shotter (1986), of the organized settings brought about by past participations acting to point to commonplaces, or affording common reference for present participation.

Within this framework, communicating that affirms this constituting role would be good communicating. Conversely, communicating that denies its own constitutiveness would be classed as bad. An excellent example of bad communication on this ground of denying constitutiveness can be found in the communication process enacted in courts of law. I have had a long-term research interest in the relationship between law and communicating because the law is such a powerful social institution for regulating our actions through language.

In previous papers (Penman, 1987a, 1987b) I have shown that the adversary system of justice relies on a model of practical reasoning that is analogous to Grice's (1975) Co-operative Principle. I also demonstrated how the words uttered by witnesses in court are taken as having a representational role only (Penman, 1991). The words are taken only as the means for establishing "facts" and these "facts" can only be specific literal truths that the person has directly experienced. There is an insistence that the words be grounded into an objective reality. The slippery nature of words and the problems that can arise when attempts are made to ground meaning into an objective reality can be illustrated in this episode from one court case.

[On examination]

Lawyer: Did Mr Fray come and live with you in the house?

Mrs Fray: Yes, he stayed and he did not stay. He had a girlfriend. Then he stayed one night with his girlfriend, one night with me.

[Cross-examination starts]

Lawyer: Would it broadly speaking be correct to say that in that period between 1957 and 1966 that you were living apart from him for about half that period in total?

Mrs Fray: I did not live. He lived. He lived 2 years with a hairdresser woman in Ainslie. Then he lived with this women what he lives with now and God knows where he lived. Ask, you ask him.

Lawyer: Mrs Fray, you have just referred to, just in your answer then, to a period of 2 years as I understand it, between 1957 and 1966 when you and Mr Fray were not living together. Could I get from you the total period of time between 1957 and 1966 when you and Mr Fray were not living together, approximately?

Mrs Fray: When we were not living together was the only time when Mr Fray was running around and living with, carrying prostitutes around or living with someone. Ask Mr Fray. He can give you more answer than I do.

This exchange was a problem for all concerned. The court requirement for an objective time measure for a relationship was incommensurate with the perspective of Mrs Fray. And, as can be seen in the extract, there was no attempt to come to terms with the meanings she wanted to attribute to it, nor to reach any understanding of it. In broad terms, the court treats the communication process as only something instrumental for the far more important legal process. This is well illustrated by a comment from one lawyer interviewed for one of my studies: "You don't converse in court, you're just asking questions and getting answers." For legal representatives, questions and answers are not conversation!

As a consequence of this peculiar role (or nonrole) given to communicating in courts, witnesses are also seen as nothing more than an instrument to be used in the legal process. Their active participation in the meaning generation process is denied, although still real. Thus, although the very process of examination and cross-examination in court acts to create a story for judgment, the court acts as if reality is being reproduced, not continually generated afresh with each act of participation. This quite clearly denies the constituting characteristic of communication.

We can also find a similar phenomenon in various theories of communication. I mentioned Grice's Co-operative Principle (1975) earlier in relation to the courtroom research I have done. Here I suggest that Grice's Co-operative Principle falls into the same trap as that demonstrated in the court episode. One of Grice's key assumptions is that people adhere to the co-operative principle in order to achieve the goal of "maximally effective exchange of information"; in other words, people co-operate with each other for efficiency of message exchange. Underlying this assumption is the belief that communication is about the exchange of information, not the generation of it. If information is exchanged, then it must also be seen as existing independent of our communicative participation. In other words, Grice implicitly assumed that information exists in its own right. In consequence, the self-generating and self-specifying features of communicating are denied by his principle.

Contextualizing

I started chapter 2 of this book with the observation that communicating always occurs in a context—both spatial and temporal—and it is the context that provides the frame for meaning generation. The context, however, is no more stable than the communication process itself. With inevitable changes in context, come changes in interpretation of communicative acts. Communicating exists in a reflexive relationship with its context. So the meaning given to any particular communicative action or episode must be seen as subject to infinite revision (Gergen, 1982). The labeling of an act at a particular point in time and in a given structural context is subject to constant revision as the retrospective and emergent contexts change with the process itself. As Gergen (1982) went on to note, the implication is that the basis for any particular description of communicative acts is not fundamentally empirical; it relies instead on a weaving of interdependent and continuously modifiable interpretations.

When meaning, or intelligibility, of action is taken to be immutable over time and/or space, then the critical feature of contextuality is denied. This is, to paraphrase Campbell (1992), a denial of historicity that flies in the face of our own humanity. In contrast, if we are to act truly, we are committed to the continual possibility of revision as we recognize the transitory nature of our understanding.

Again, clear examples of the denial of context can be found in courts of law. The language game imposed by the courts assumes that the meaning of an act talked about in court is the same meaning of the act when it occurred in time past. This is illustrated in the common insistence of the court that the witness repeat or say exactly what happened at the time of the incidence under question—as if any retelling produces the same intelligibility as at the time past. Consider the following example from a court case (note a slash, /, indicates the witness was cut off):

> *Lawyer:* At the time when you handed the document to the accused, concerning his new position as finance officer, did you say anything to him about his obligations with regard to your company?
>
> *Witness:* Yes. He would have been told specifically/
>
> *Lawyer:* Not what you would have, what you said.
>
> *Witness:* I would have told him that his/
>
> *Judge:* No, no. Do not please say "I would have told him", say "I did something" or "I said something."

What is interesting about this example is the insistence that events in the past must, and can, be talked about in the present as if they had not changed with the context. This example also illustrates how the court assumes it can make sense of a reported utterance without considering the context of what the other person said. In both instances, there is a denial of the contextualizing nature of communicating and thus further evidence of bad communicating.

Diversity

The continually creative and continually modifying nature of communicating means that there is a great diversity to communicating, or in our interpretations of it. Given, that there is no empirical base to any interpretation, the possibilities are endless. The ontic status of any communicative act lies only in the description, not in the act itself. As such, there can be as many descriptions as we, in our participation, are capable of generating.

In a very broad and almost paradoxical sense we could suggest that better descriptions/interpretations are those that recognize the diversity that is possible. More specifically, we could also suggest that any claim to there being one and only one right interpretation is a bad way of communicating. Perhaps the most commonly experienced form of this bad communication is found in marital arguments that proceed from bad to worse on the assumption that each partner's different claim to interpretation is the only correct one.

Better descriptions/interpretations also need to recognize that there are no objective, outside grounds on which to make a claim that any one interpretation is superior to another. It is not possible to say that this interpretation is better than another one because it is more real. As there is no objective base to interpretation, there are no objective grounds on which to make the claim. We are unable to appeal to fact and, instead, must inexorably return to value. We may wish to say that this interpretation is better than another, but can only do so on nonfactual grounds, such as moral or aesthetic ones. Unfortunately, this does not happen in the case of marital arguments cited earlier.

A very different but fundamentally important example of the denial of diversity can be found in the imposition of a standard language across diverse cultures. The imposition of English in this regard can only be seen as an extreme example of imperialism. Although it may well ease the so-called "communication barriers", at the same time it oppresses or eliminates our diverse options for understanding. Languages are, in fact, a major source of cultural wealth for humanity, and diversity in languages needs to be encouraged rather than minimized. The work of some linguistics in recording and documenting the vast range of languages in the Pacific is an important example of productive work in this regard (e.g., Mühlhäusler, 1988)

The requirement of encouraging diversity also has important ramifications for communication theory. As Craig (1999) argued in his proposal for reconstructing communication theory as a field, we should not be striving for a unified theory of communication. Indeed, the very practice of communicating, with its endlessly evolving ways, makes such a search for unity and coherence futile. Instead, "[t]he goal . . . should be the very condition that Dance (1970) was so keen to avoid: theoretical diversity, argument, debate, even at the cost of occasional lapses into academic sniping" (Craig, 1999, pp. 123–4).

In addition, I would like to suggest that diversity should be encouraged, not just of theories or accounts but within theories or accounts. Rather than develop a theory or account that specifies one basis for action or one possibility for it, we need to develop a range of possibilities by which we might account for action. As part of this, we should consider the moral task of creating new languages or ways of understanding. Sless argued repeatedly for this need: "If we are to deepen and enlarge our understanding of the human condition and the world, our arts and sciences need to be constantly revitalised by new means of expression; progress depends on our capacity to create new models, metaphors and analogies" (Sless, 1986, p. 154).

With this approach to theory and language development, the link between theory and practice is not via experimentation, as the conventional scientific pathway has it. Instead, there is a direct link between conceptual matters and the structure of everyday life. We need to be concerned with specifying the possibilities open to us in talk about communicating, such that we might choose to realize them in practice.

Incompleteness

The meanings generated in communicating are never complete or even capable of being finished. In continually bringing about a new state of affairs, joint participations and the implicated meanings are always emergent and never finished. Meanings are always vague possibilities. Sless (1986) made a very poignant remark about the unfinished nature of meaning and understanding: "Understanding is the dead spot in our struggle for meaning; it is the momentary pause, the stillness before incomprehension continues" (1986, p .i). This is not to suggest the possibility that meaning could be complete, if only . . . . On the contrary, meanings are essentially unfinishable.

Underlying this proposition is the recognition that disorder and chaos are at the base of social life. This recognition, however, does not have to lead us to the nihilistic position of the deconstructionists (e.g., Derrida, 1977). From their perspective, all attempts at discovering underlying order must inevitably fail, and therefore there is no point in attempting such a search. However, from the perspective developed here, while the search for an underlying order is pointless, the imposition of order onto chaos is not.

In principle, the meanings implicated in communicating are always indeterminate, but they are not wholly treated so in practice. We have the capacity for creating order out of the potential chaos of indeterminacy. The "organized settings" (Shotter, 1986) we are led into by our past acts of participation and implicated meanings serve as constraints on the range of possibilities. These constraints provide temporary closure in an otherwise unstable and indeterminate social world. In this way, although there is the potential for an infinite range of meanings, in practice this is limited by the closure we impose. The issue then becomes one not of determining (or even believing in) the stability of meaning, but instead of studying the points of and procedures for closure.

In general, good communicating recognizes the open-endedness of communicating. This was the major thrust of Rorty's (1980) arguments, leading to his injunction that the moral task of the philosopher or social critic is to defend the openness of human conversation. It is also the major thrust underlying developments in the area of argumentation. Michael Billig's (1987) treatise on *Arguing and Thinking* brought this issue to the fore. As he pointed out, the biggest gap in modern psychological (and social) theories concerns their lack of attention to argumentation. By *argumentation*, Billig meant the rhetorical process of debating for and against propositions; a process that, in ancient times, was seen to be at the center of human affairs (Billig, 1987).

In part, we could attribute this lack of attention to argumentation to a preoccupation with a converse concept—co-operation. A co-operative base is frequently assumed in theories of our social activities, especially the more linguistically based ones (e.g., Grice, 1975). It is also assumed in some earlier developments within the constructionist framework being used here. For example, Gergen (1985, p. 267) maintained that "the process of understanding is the result of an active, co-operative enterprise of persons in relationships." The concept of co-operation used in such claims assumes that people choose to willingly work together in a mutual enterprise to bring about a mutual benefit—in the instance of Gergen's claim, this is shared understanding.

However, this assumption of co-operation is not necessary (Penman, 1988). Understanding of some form or another is still possible in active, unco-operative participation. Moreover, if we are to assume that co-operation is necessary, we are unable to account for the substantive role played by the argumentative or controversial dimension in our social life. Good communicating does not have to be co-operative. Indeed, it could be the case that many co-operative efforts lead to a premature closure of the conversation, with the result that a full range of possible options are not explored or diversity encouraged. From Rorty's (1980) point of view it is far more important to keep the argument going than to finish it. The importance of keeping the argument going formed part of the challenge to Habermas' requirement of rational consensus (Bernstein, 1983); rational consensus being potentially counterproductive to continuing argumentation and debate.

This leads us to an interesting position. Although emphasizing the importance of keeping the argument going, there are very good practical reasons to impose some form of closure, and quite narrow ones in some instances. A good example in point is the closure imposed on our interpretation of traffic lights: It would be unwise for us to maintain an argument about the meaning of red and green lights at road intersections. We could extend this analogy into communicating practice where, similarly, it would be unwise to maintain an openness of interpretation while a spouse engages in repeated domestic violence. Lines must be drawn, for some practical reasons at least.

In general, some form of closure, however temporary, is needed for the maintenance of our everyday social life. On the other hand, other forms of closure may well curtail that very same social life. This raises the question of which points of closure are premature and which forms of closure are too limiting. Interestingly, in exploring this question, I am led back to a consideration of aesthetics and acting truly. In chapter 4, I described an aesthetic experience as a momentary understanding of the pattern, structure, and coherence of an experience. An aesthetic judgment is a momentary point of closure. I also suggested that a good aesthetic judgment is always open to revision. Good closure, then, is characterized by being momentary and open to change. The open-endedness of communicating is recognized, while momentary pauses for comprehension—for closure—allow us to go on. Here I argue that it is the practical experience of being able to go on that it is the critical test of good closure.

Some forms of communicating simply fail to recognize this open-endedness, and those forms can be classed as bad. Theories and practice that presume the possibility of perfect understanding could be placed in this category. In assuming that perfect understanding is possible, the ongoingness and unfinishability of the meaning generation process is denied. Other practices that presume there is one and only one meaning possible (usually that of the believer in one meaning) also fall into this category of bad communicating.

On the other hand, those theories and practices that have no closure, when the practical exigencies of the world seem to call for it, are equally bad. There is a tendency in arguments of this kind and within the constructionist constellation to be too open, and this brings its own problems. Although we might want to respect all opinions and theories there may be very good practical reasons why we should not. The right to hold any opinion may be sustainable, but the implications for practice cannot always be supported morally. In the end, I cannot morally support a theory that has an impoverished representation of the human experience and that, in practice, negates a range of possible actions for improving the human condition.

◄ℚ Using the criteria

In making the three discontinuous leaps in the last three chapters, I have been led to reconsider the very basis of evaluation itself. What is perhaps important to emphasize here is that I have not rejected any form of evaluation. I have not said any and all meaning constructions are acceptable, or are as good as one another. I have not been forced into the ultimate relativist's position that no judgment is possible. That would be to fall into the trap of no closure at all. Instead, I have gone beyond the objectivist-relativist dichotomy into another realm altogether; one in which it is recognised that judgments can and should be made on good moral grounds.

These four criteria for making judgments are offered as a way that we, as momentary observers (or authors) of communicating or accounts of it, can make an aesthetic assessment with moral import. They are criteria that can only be used in the authorial position (to use Bakhtin's phrase). Our overriding concern in using these criteria to make judgments is to display good faith with the communicating process we are judging.

This is a far cry from the conventional form of judgments used in communication research and practice. In everyday practice, we are most likely to make judgments in terms of how well our acts accomplished what we wanted. As a I discussed at the beginning of this chapter, this is also a common research judgment. Such conventional judgments are premised on a world view that assumes an instrumental notion of communication (noun form) and that denies or ignores the very process of communicating.

Instead of making judgments about things outside of the process, I have argued that we make the judgments from within, in terms of the extent to which the process or the theory affirms four characteristics of communicating: constituting, contextualizing, diverisifying and incompleteness. This is not an easy process, nor one that is intuitively obvious. I have given some examples of communication processes and theories that fall short in affirming each of these characteristics. But to round off here and provide some temporary closure, I will extend the court examples used earlier to maintain that courtroom communication practices, relying on the adversarial system of justice, falls short on all four criteria.

I have already described how the courts treat words as if they have only a representational role and are of relevance only in establishing the facts. This, of course, presumes a truth independent of the words used to describe it. As such, the discourse rules of courtroom examination and cross-examination deny the constituting characteristic of communicating. Similarly, by insisting on an immutable reality (that events in the past can be talked about in the present as if they had not changed with the context) the contextualizing feature is denied. In much the same way, the discourse rules of court deny the diversity of interpretations and the inevitable incompleteness of our understandings. Indeed, the very need for legal certainty forces such a denial.

Within the legal institutional frame, communication is simply a tool for legal ends, and so are the people in the process. However, in order to force this purely instrumental role onto the situation, the court has to use a number of coercive devices, from direct admonitions (as demonstrated in the earlier examples) to threats of contempt of court (see Penman, 1987b). In fact, in the courtroom research I talked about earlier, it became obvious that ordinary citizens on the witness stand could not readily follow the legal discourse rules; the requirements were unnatural for them. The most unnatural part of the whole process was the denial of the relational aspects of the process and, more broadly, its contextual features—what I called the "face game" (Penman, 1991).

Looking at the communication practices in court in this way provides the basis for a critical reconsideration of the judicial process based on the adversary system. In general, my analyses and arguments led me to the conclusion that the process of justice enacted in the adversary system neither facilitates the establishment of the facts of the case nor ensures a just hearing in the best possible manner. The facts established are severely distorted because the court ignores the critical role of context and the constituting process in which the so-called facts are determined. Moreover, the court's formal rules of discourse and the adversary process combined to treat all witnesses as worthy of contempt. They are treated contemptuously because the critical role of relationship negotiation (face game) is denied while an atypical mode of communicating is imposed on those witnesses.

It is quite extraordinary when you do look at courtroom communicating in this way and realize that it is an exemplar form of bad communicating, at least from within the language game developing here. It is also a particularly amoral form; one that, to use Campbell's words (1992) "flies in the face of our own humanity" by renouncing historicity and attempting to construct an impersonal timeless account of reality. By way of contrast, in the next chapter, I consider an exemplar form of good communicating.

6

The possibility of dialogue

In chapter 2, I described three alternatives to the conventional wisdom that the process of communication is inessential, or immaterial, and laid out the choice I'm taking in this book: to deny the conventional wisdom and assert that communicating is material. I also pointed out that one of the important consequences of choosing this third option is its implications for practice. When communicating is taken as material, we are able to recognize the critical role it plays in our understandings of and acting into our world. With this recognition we are hopefully also able to directly face the practical concerns of our world and, from the position of participation, ask what can we do.

In chapters 3, 4 and 5, I elaborated a conceptual framework, a way of talking about communicating as material that can help in asking questions of "What can we do?" The last chapter also explored how we can make judgments about these doings; how we can say if we are doing things well. This exploration was premised on a proposition of Campbell's: "If we are to act truly, our approach to entities in the worlds must maintain an open attitude, so that we *let them show themselves as they are*" (1992, p. 425, emphasis added). From this I proceeded to show how an open approach to communicating allowed us to affirm the characteristics of itself—constituting, contextualizing, diversifying, and ongoing.

In this chapter I want to build further on this proposal by discussing a particular form of communicating that exemplifies a self-affirming process—dialogue. In chapter 3, I briefly introduced this notion of dialogue as one descriptor for the present continuous form of communicating; where the focus is on the process, and the outcome is not prefigured. Now I want to use it as an example of good communicating.

Note that the chapter title includes the word *possibility*. Before we proceed any further, I want to emphasize that this word is important. Dialogue is not necessarily something that we would want to achieve all the time, nor would it be possible to do so. I do not want the following discussion to be taken as advocating that we should strive to achieve dialogue all the time, in all contexts. Instead, I want to argue that it is a possibility immanent in the practice of communicating that we could perhaps aspire to more often than we do now. To make more sense of this, let's turn to what the notion of dialogue can mean.

⟪Q Understandings of dialogue

The concept of dialogue has been used in a number of different ways, and interest in it has grown in many disciplines across the human sciences. Indeed, as Cissna and Anderson (1998) argued, scholarship in this area is so extensive that it is difficult to comprehensively review all the material (nor is it necessary here, there being many recent comprehensive anthologies). One of the more useful review collections is Anderson, Cissna and Arnett's (1994) *The Reach of Dialogue: Confirmation, Voice, and Community*. In the first chapter of that collection, Cissna and Anderson (1994) reviewed the various traditions of dialogue. They suggested that there are at least four relatively distinct, although not unrelated, traditions of dialogue that co-exist in the contemporary literature. More recently, Stewart and Zediker (1999) made a useful distinction between traditions that offer descriptive accounts and those that offer prescriptive ones.

The need to make distinctions between types of accounts of dialogues was brought home quite vividly at the 1999 International Communication Association Conference in San Francisco. Given my interest, I attended every session with the word *dialogue* in its title and discovered that there were almost as many different usages of the word as sessions held. What I also discovered was that there was a tendency to use the concept in such a general way that it was simply a synonym for human contact or for conversation: Dialogue (automatically) occurs in a face-to-face interaction between two or more people. The concept has been used in this way in a range of conversational and discourse analysis approaches (e.g., Tannen, 1989). It has also been used similarly in the ergonomic literature, where there is an increasing body of research literature on human–computer dialogue. In this instance, *dialogue* is used synonymously with *interaction* between the human and the computer (e.g., Salvendy, 1987).

I am not interested in using *dialogue* in this overgeneralized way here. It serves no purpose if it is taken as simply meaning the same as *conversation* or *communication*. Rather, I want to suggest that it needs to take on a specific, differentiating meaning. The distinction between descriptive and prescriptive accounts made by Stewart and Zediker (1999) offers a choice: between using dialogue as a descriptor for a particular way of looking at communication/human interaction, or as a prescriptor for a particular way of being in communicating.

Descriptive approaches are concerned with pointing to an irreducible aspect of social life: its inherent dialogic character. Bakhtin is widely acknowledged as one of the leading proponents of this descriptive view,; although you should bear in mind that Bakhtin himself used the concept in different ways. Morson and Emerson (1989) maintained that his different usages can be distilled into two distinct senses. In one, all of language use is essentially dialogical as it orients to a listener. In the other sense, only some of language use is dialogical—when it exploits the play of contexts and voices and encourages 'social acts' of engagement between people (or authors and readers, to use Bakhtin's terms). The communication literature has typically relied on Bakhtin's first sense—that all language is essentially dialogical. Interestingly, however, some have blended his two senses. For example, Montgomery and Baxter (1998) did so when they used dialogic to contrast with dualistic and monologic views of personal relationships. For them, "[d]ialogic approaches, including relational dialectics, implicate a kind of in-the-moment, interactive multivocality, in which multiple points of view retain their integrity as they play off each other" (Montgomery & Baxter, 1998, p. 185).

The work of Hans-Georg Gadamer (1992) and other hermaneuticians can also be seen as falling into this descriptive approach. For them, dialogue stands for a way of thinking and questioning in the relationship between the interpreter and the text. Gadamer's central work on *Truth and Method* (which I made use of in chapter 4) is essentially about a dialogic conception of knowledge. In that work he argued that the processes involved in spoken dialogue reflect exactly the task of hermeneutics—that of entering into a dialogue with the text. Importantly, he pointed to a central characteristic of this dialogic process—a truth emerges that is neither yours or mine, but arises out of our joint action. In every "true conversation . . . each person opens himself to the other and truly accepts his point of view as valid" (Gadamer, 1992, p. 385).

Similarly, Shotter (1993) wrote about the role of joint action in negotiating understandings; although here Shotter drew far more on a Wittgensteinian-Bakhtinian perspective than an hermeneutical one. Shotter uses phrases like "the dialogical, joint nature of human activity" (1997c, p. 3) or the "dialogical, relational-responsive view of language use" (1998a, p. 185) to point to a particular way of looking at, or talking about, human social activity. This activity, he argued, occurs in a sphere of joint action, a world of its own that is outside of causality or human action. It is a zone of indeterminancy (Shotter, 1997c).

I have actually been using this descriptive approach to dialogue in my arguments in the chapters to date. In particular, I have drawn on the works of Shotter, Gadamer, and Bakhtin. However, I have not actually used the word *dialogue* to emphasize the relational, joint nature of humans; instead, I chose to use the word *communicating*. This is not to deny the value of these descriptive approaches to dialogue or the importance I place on the arguments; rather it is because I want to reserve the word dialogue for a specific, prescriptive purpose.

Stewart and Zediker described the prescriptive approaches to dialogue as identifying "features of contact that are not always present, may not always be desirable, and are not always possible, but that can serve as an ideal toward which communication may fruitfully move" (1999, p. 6). In this approach, dialogue is a special form of communicating that is qualitatively different from other forms. In addition, prescriptive approaches share a concern to bring about change in communicating practice, not just describe it in a particular way. However, even in these prescriptive approaches, differences can be discerned. Here I draw on two of the more popular traditions: those influenced by the work of Buber (e.g., 1958) and of Bohm (e.g., 1996).

In Buber's view, all forms of human life are relational, but dialogue stands for a particular kind or quality of relating with the other—the I-Thou relation. This kind of relating is an ideal; not something that could always be achieved, but something to strive for as much as possible, given what the resources and the situation allow. Dialogue occurs when there is a genuine meeting with the other (Buber, 1958). For Buber, there is a special emphasis on the quality of relating in terms of a way of being with the other person in dialogue.

In contrast, Bohm described dialogue as a process of thinking (cf. relating) together, that makes the participants "share in a common 'meaning pool' which lays the foundations for taking coherent action together" (Ellinor & Gerard, 1998, p. 38). Dialogue is the method for going beyond individual consciousness into mutual communing in order to perceive reality correctly. Dialogue is to be encouraged because it is a means to learn of, and perceive, a larger reality.

Pearce and Pearce (1999) have analysed the communication characteristics of a dialogue session informed by the Buber tradition (the Cupertino Diversity Forum) and one run along Bohmian lines (a partnership dialogue reported in Ellinor & Gerard, 1998). Drawing on Pearce's (1989) typology of different forms of communication, they described the partnership dialogue as a form of modernistic communication, and the diversity forum as cosmopolitan. They went on to note that the different traditions of practice found in modernistic and cosmopolitan communication reflect striking differences in their concept and evaluation of communication. The Bohmian dialogue tradition, reflecting a modernistic communication form, sees communication as a means of describing reality and transmitting messages about it: "Communication is a secondary process serving other, more important functions, such as perception, thought, and collective action" (Pearce & Pearce, 1999, p. 21). In contrast, the tradition of the diversity forum, reflecting a cosmopolitan communication form, is explicitly based on a social constructionist perspective: "The purpose of dialogue, from this perspective, is not to overcome the specific limitations of our experience but to create communication patterns that valorize and allow the expression of even incommensurate cultures, histories and values" (Pearce & Pearce, 1999, p. 21).

Clearly, the Buberian tradition of dialogue is the most compatible with the framework I am using here, and it is this I shall draw on as I proceed with the chapter. I wish to treat dialogue as a particular form of practice that reflects what Pearce (1989) calls "cosmopolitan" communicating. It is a form of communicating that is oriented to the relationship between participants, in particular ways. It is a form that only happens sometimes. But, despite the infrequent occurrence of dialogue, we still need to recognize the possibility that dialogue is immanent in all our communication practices. I made a similar argument in the last chapter as the grounds for developing criteria for evaluating communicating. There, I said that the ideals for good communicating being posited by certain theorists (e.g., Habermas & Arendt) are somehow already immanent in the communicating community. The possibility is there, but it is not necessarily realized in practice (Bernstein, 1983). This is also the case with dialogue, as a particular form of communicating. And, as a particular form it is not a thing, as in the entity/noun form, but instead a practice as in the gerund/verb form. So, as with the arguments for communicating I now want to turn to a consideration of dialoguing.

When we come to pinning dialoguing down definitionally, however, it becomes just that little bit more tricky, because of the very thing we are trying to make it be—an ongoing, open process. Cissna and Anderson (1994) also noted this trickiness: "In dialogue, we do not know exactly what we are going to say, and we can surprise not only the other but even ourselves because we may say something, as Buber put it, 'we haven't said [or thought] before'." (p. 10). Here they are referring to a conversation, in which the moderator of a "public dialogue" between Carl Rogers and Martin Buber asked Buber how he would know if he had done his job tonight. Buber responded, "If either Carl or I says something that we haven't said before, we'll know that it's a success" (Kirschenbaum & Henderson, 1989, p. 185).

I find this both particularly poignant and apt. It provides a key, as it were, for helping distinguish dialoguing from other conversational practices. Dialoguing accomplishes new things. In dialoguing we open new possibilities. This suggests important links back to the discussions on the moral dimensions of communicating and the essentially open-ended characteristic of communicating. If, as I said in chapter 5, we are to engage in good communicating, we must recognize this open-endedness.

Others, coming from different starting points, have also written of the importance of openness and its relation to new possibilities. For example, Bennett (1985) made an important argument regarding communication and social responsibility, in which he concluded that good communication keeps language sensitive and accountable to human experience and, by implication, keeps our experiences open. A similar theme was reflected in Klaus Krippendorff's (1989) essay on the ethics of communication. He argued that we have a major social imperative: "In communicating with others, maintain or expand the range of choices possible" (p. 93). In this maintenance or expansion of the choices offered we enable the people with whom we are participating to go on. The question now is: How can this be done? What practices need to be realised for the possibility of dialoguing to become an actuality?

◖ Dialoguing

Everyone I know who advocates a prescriptive approach to dialoguing would assert that there are no hard and fast rules for ensuring that the practice of dialoguing emerges. Dialoguing cannot be done by following a set of injunctions or by applying technical knowledge (see chapter 4). It is something that happens between people, and no one person can be in control. Even with the good intent of all participants, a pattern of dialoguing will not necessarily emerge. Nevertheless, good intent and and a certain orientation to the conversation are still essential prerequisites.

Cissna and Anderson (1994) suggested that there are eight characteristics that can be drawn from a merging of the different traditions, although they recognize that not all writers on the subject would subscribe equally to them. Although I find these eight characteristics useful, what drives me here is a consideration of how communicating needs to be practiced to accomplish new things and to open up new possibilities. I want to consider four features of such a practice, from the point of view of what we, as participants, should be doing to engage in this practice.

As we proceed, I hope it becomes apparent that the practices I describe allow the four features of good communicating discussed in chapter 5 to "show themselves as they are" (Campbell, 1992, p. 425). In chapter 5, I described these features from the perspective of the process. In this chapter, the descriptions are from the perspective of the participants in the process. However, the four features of the process discussed in chapter 5 should not be taken as being equivalent to each of the four practices to be described here—it is purely fortuitous that there are four in each set of descriptions. Instead, the four features described here are the requirements for collectively allowing the development of a self-affirming process that recognizes its constituting, contextualizing, diversifying, and ongoing characteristics.

Engaging in, acting authentically

Being truly engaged in communicating is one of the four prerequisites for the possibility of dialogue. This was the key point that Buber (1965) made when he drew a distinction between "being" and "seeming"—a distinction that I find very useful, mainly because so many people in conversations seem to be seeming. The being persons offer themselves, as it were, to the others with no concern about how the others are seeing them. There is no concern with impression management here! On the other hand, the seeming persons are mainly concerned with what others think of them, and produce looks to make them appear to be spontaneous, sincere, or whatever else they think is desirable. Seeming persons are not participating in, they are impressing on.

This distinction helps me account for why I find so much of public discourse frustrating and undesirable. As an example, consider the public debates and discussions generated for television current affairs and documentaries. I always get the sense that the interviewer and interviewee are "seeming" and not "being." The whole interaction is oriented to the appearance of the thing; they are performances in which nothing new can possibly emerge. The fabricated nature prohibits dialoguing.

A similar phenomenon can be found in many public consultation processes between governments and citizens. Consider, for example, the community hall filled with irate citizens complaining about some development. Typically, at the front of the hall (and up on a dais) are government representatives running the meeting. Are they really engaging in a process or simply defending their position, with no possibility for change? Are they really being in the conversation, or just seeming to be? More often than not these meetings simply perpetuate a polarized conflict that does nothing to meet community needs.

The point is that an engagement in communicating is an essential prerequisite for the possibility of dialoguing. On the other hand, only seeming to do so, precludes that very same possibility. If you are only concerned with how you seem to be, it is not possible to fully participate in communicating.

This notion of "being" has also been referred to as acting authentically or honestly. For example, Cissna and Anderson (1994) argued that "[t]he ground of dialogue is the presumption of honesty" (p. 15). What is important here is that the participants operate on the presumption of honesty, without needing to discover if the other is authentic or not. You do not need to ask "Is that true?", you proceed as if it were. I have a little trouble with using the word *honesty* here, because it often connotes the notion of truth that I discussed and dismissed in chapter 4. Instead I reintroduce Campbell's (1992) notion of acting in good faith, and suggest that one of the grounds for dialoguing requires acting faithfully into the situation. It also requires the presumption of good faith on the part of other participants. Without this good faith, this authenticity to the process, dialoguing is not possible.

It is perhaps important to emphasize here, that when I use the phrase *acting authentically* it is in reference to the process, not the self. The need to make this distinction was brought home clearly in the email conversation in which I participated leading up to the 1999 International Communication Conference panel on "Taking Dialogue Seriously: Maintaining Difference and Creating Common Ground." In that preconference conversation, it was pointed out that authenticity had troublesome Cartesian implications to do with presumed notions of a real self to whom one could be authentic. This is incommensurate with the framework here. Yet, it is still possible and useful to conceive of a form of authenticity that is oriented to the process, not a self. However, this orientation is of a particular form. As Bob Kreisher suggested, in our email discussions, the particular orientation to temporality can be used to distinguish between authenticity and inauthenticity. Authenticity is present when we are acting into the conversational moment. In contrast, authenticity is not present when we are acting instrumentally (in order to) or retrospectively (objectifying).

Future orientation, going with the flow

I started chapter 2 with the idea of context in the verb form, where meaning is generated from the mutual interplay of context and utterance. In the last chapter, I discussed the contexuality of communicating as one of its essential characteristics. Our understandings, at any point in time and in any structural context, are subject to constant revision because the retrospective and emergent contexts change with the process of communicating itself.

Communicating essentially occurs over time—it is a process that goes on. This temporal context was critical for Freire (Shor & Freire, 1987), who said that dialogue had to be understood as something that occurred in the very historical nature of human beings. Campbell (1992), for different reasons, also focused on this historicity. Renouncing this historicity is acting in bad faith: "An impersonal and timeless account of reality [that] flies in the face of our own humanity" (p. 438). As part of our acting authentically to the process, then, we need to be open and sensitive to the temporal context of the process in which we are engaging. We need to recognize that our understanding can and does change as the process proceeds.

For me, the critical element of this recognition is the idea that, in setting the ground for dialogue, we are future orientated. Dewey's (1981) pragmatic arguments about this future orientation are useful here. Dewey maintained that it is not the antecedent phenomena or the precedents that are critical to our understandings, but instead the consequent phenomena and the possibilities for future action. In Dewey's framework, "Anticipation is more primary than recollection, projection more than a summoning of the past, the prospective more than the retrospective" (Rogers, 1994, p. 41).

However, I would like to extend Dewey's argument further. Rather than just saying that the prospective is more important than the retrospective, I would also like to argue that one precludes the other, at least when dialoguing. You cannot be looking back—to contemplate antecedents—while you are looking forward—to understanding possibilities—within the same communication process. This would be like two people with their backs to each other trying to row a boat, each pulling in the opposing direction. Just as it would be impossible for them to move, so would it be impossible for genuine participators to move if they started to look backwards, while still in participation. Looking backward always loses the moment; the momentum of conversations is forward. In looking forward we are presented with the unfolding of options and the closing off of others as the constructive activity proceeds.

Dialoguing needs this future orientation toward the momentary order of possibilities—the permissions or affordings—that are offered as a conversation proceeds. Similarly, we need to be oriented to what options are closed as we proceed, and how we can go on regardless. This is a view from within the process; within the practice of communicating. It is an orientation to going on, and generating the means to do so (hopefully well). It is view oriented to future solutions or possibilities, not to past causes of problems. However, I want to emphasize that I do not think it is enough, as some have argued, simply to keep the conversation going (e.g., Rorty, 1980). Conversations can go round in circles and can go backwards, often in weird paradoxical loops and often seemingly forever. What is important is that the conversation goes forward into new things, not just continues.

Collaborating, mutually

Working to go on and to keep the possibilities open, also requires a commitment to mutual collaboration. Individuals acting singularly do not keep the process going; it continues through the mutual, collaborative effort of all. To participate well, this mutuality also needs to be affirmed. However, we need to consider here exactly what can be meant by *mutuality*. For some, mutuality means equal contribution (e.g., Habermas in McCarthy, 1984). This way of understanding mutuality presumes a whole range of contextual factors, including equality of capacities, powers, and so on. But I do not think we need or want to make these assumptions here. Indeed, as Cissna and Anderson (1998) pointed out, no relationship could ever exhibit complete equality. Yet, this should not preclude some sort of a mutual process.

Instead, then, I suggest that mutuality can simply mean that all participants are committed and able to make some contribution to the process. In particular, they need to be able to contribute to the joint development of the methods by which new understandings and changes are brought about. This is what Cissna and Anderson (1994) referred to as a commitment to "the joint project of sense-making" (p. 14). It also reflects the arguments of Bennett (1985) I mentioned earlier, in which good communicating increases "the chances of ordinary people to participate in the discovery and transformation of their own condition" (p. 259).

In this view, mutuality is expressed by the nature and quality of the contributions that the participants in the process make. These are contributions that allow all participants to jointly create new understandings and possibilities of importance to them. It is perhaps pertinent to point out that this form of mutuality is only possible when all participants are acting in good faith, or being authentic to the process.

Here, I am clearly using the concept of mutuality as a reflection of what participants contribute to the process. In contrast, mutuality also been considered as a momentary apprehension of the other and self in dialogue. This is the sense that Carl Rogers talked about in his dialogue with Martin Buber. The periods of mutuality "are the moments in which the relationship is experienced the same on both sides" (Cissna & Anderson, 1998, p. 71). This sense is not incompatible with the first and both may be usefully treated together. With all participants collaborating in a commitment to sense-making, by jointly developing the means to do so, moments of mutuality are more likely to emerge.

Presence, immediacy

I cannot imagine being authentic, future-orientated, and collaborating, without being in the physical presence of the other(s). There are good reasons for arguing that it is an essential requirement for dialoguing and these reasons rely on arguments introduced in Chapter 4. There, I talked about the concept of morally knowing, drawing on the work of Gadamer (1992) and Shotter (1993). Moral knowing does not exist independently of the social situation; it is brought about within it. In discussing this concept I drew on Shotter's example of the sense of obligation we feel once we are in the physical presence of another and acknowledge that presence: "It is only from within this obligation that we can . . . fully experience . . . reality through the ethical relations established in our initial acknowledgments" (Shotter, 1997a, p. 7).

In that same chapter, I also discussed Bauman's (1991) account of the social manipulation of morality. He argued that social organization is able to neutralize the impact of moral action through three complementary arrangements. One of these arrangements is particularly pertinent here. Those who may feel the moral import of another's actions are kept away from the presence of the other, or denied any encountering space. In this way they never need to see a human face (or hear a human voice) that "might become visible and glare as a moral demand" (Bauman, 1991, p. 145).

In their different ways, both Shotter and Bauman are arguing for an integral relationship between physical presence or embodiment and the moral obligations that ensue. It is only when we are in the physical presence of an other(s) that the moral demand of the engagement continues to pull us forward, as it were. Thus, physical presence generates an immediacy for action. It is in the immediacy of the moment that demands are made to continue. If we recognize those demands and are committed to meeting them, then dialoguing becomes more possible.

Dewey's argument for the recovery of experience (see chapter 3) also provides good grounds for the essentialness of physical presence. When we orient ourselves to experience, it leads us directly to the real world of embodied persons (Cronen, 1995b). It is only in our embodiment that we can experience the reality in which we exist. So, it is this sense of being embodied and physically present with another that sets a condition for the possibility of genuine engagement, mutuality, and commitment to that other.

This need for embodiment or physical presence raises challenging questions for the possibility of dialogue in cyberspace conversations. I have been

involved in various on-line conversations about dialogue since 1995, conversing with others vitally interested and involved in dialogue and have not yet
experienced or observed any dialogic moments. Although I believe we need to
be actually present with another, I will remain open on the possibility of a
virtual dialogue. Perhaps with a longer history of conversing this way we may
evolve other ways of implicating the moral demand that arises out of embodied presence.

❧ Dialoguing as practical inquiry

All of the characteristics and descriptions of dialoguing just discussed are
based on a particular way of being in relation to the other(s) in conversation.
However, so far this way of being has been described in general terms. Can we
get any closer to a description of the process, without actually engaging in it?
Perhaps we can, if we consider the very basic things that go on in conversations—listening and talking. But, of course, it needs to be a particular way of
listening and talking.

Pearce and Pearce (1999) and Stewart and Zediker (1999) described this
particular way as standing in the tension between holding your own ground
as a listener and talker and being profoundly open to the other as a listener
and talker. Engaging in this primary dynamic calls for all of the characteristics
of dialogue described in the previous section. For example, Pearce and Pearce
(1999) wrote that holding your own ground requires displays of genuineness,
openness, and reflexive awareness. You need to be aware of and acknowledge
your own ground and the logical forces at work in the conversation. Being
profoundly open to the other requires displays of acceptance, curiosity, creativity, and presentness. You need to acknowledge that others have a ground of
their own which probably is, and should be, different from yours and show a
commitment to hear and help the others' voices.

As Stewart and Zediker (1999) pointed out, understanding the process of
holding your own ground is easy for moderns and Westerners because of its
connection with the modernistic concept of the individual self. On the other
hand, the other moment in the primary dynamic—being profoundly open to
the other—is much more difficult to grasp. This moment is of primary concern
for me here; because of both its neglect and its direct relevance to ensuing

chapters in which I shall develop a mode of practical inquiry based on dialoguing as an exemplar form.

Dialogic listening and questioning

Almost by definition, communicating requires some process of listening and talking. It is this very same process that forms the basis of any practical inquiry. When we want to understand, we listen and we talk, or we read and we interrogate. However, to set up the possibility for dialoguing, our listening and talking needs to be done in relation to the other in a particular way: a way that lets the other happen to us. Here, the process of listening is critical. As Gurevitch (1989, p. 166) noted, "The problem associated with dialogue is that of overcoming the tendency to not listen, which results from seeking to understand before listening and from imposing a complete set of meanings on the situation in an effort to define it as exclusive." Good listening, then, requires an open ear—an openness to new possibilities—as well as a profound openness to the other.

However, it also requires a little more than just openness to what the other is saying. John Stewart (1990) has written extensively on a notion of dialogic listening that requires an orientation to what the conversational partners are sculpting together. The orientation is to be out there, between them, not to what is going on in the listener's head (recognizing that for the metaphor it is). With John Stewart's kind permission, I have reproduced his description (with some minor amendments for coherency) of what it feels like to engage in dialogic listening (from an e-mail, 27 August 1996), because it seems to poignantly capture the experience of it:

> As I listen dialogically, the shift in focus is palpable—from behavioral rehearsal, planning and choosing words, to what? Well, I notice that I often repeat some of the other's key words and phrases. I notice that I orient openly with all parts of my body and am aware of my being. I notice that I feel like a CO-sculptor or CO-producer, which means neither simply at the mercy of or subject to the other's idea/feeling movement NOR simply working out of my own agenda, but actually CO-Co-laborating. I notice that almost every time I am surprised. Something happens as my awareness meets the other's talk. I notice that I feel laser-focused, so that outside events recede or disappear in the face of the movement of meaning my conversation partner and I are working together on. Because of this intensity of focus, I notice that I get tired if I

stay at this for too long. I almost always notice that I have to tend to my too-natural inclination to respond defensively. This is another signal to me that the labor-ating is CO. I ain't in control, and I have sometime to resist not liking that.

This form of dialogic listening, involving "CO-Co-labor-ating" with the other, is an example of a form of experience that Gadamer (1992) referred to as *Erfahrung*: the kind of experience that happens to one in the process of practical knowing that I discussed in chapter 4. It is, to use Gadamer's phrase, a "hermeneutical experience of the Thou" (1992, p. 358). However, it is a particular experience of the Thou. Gadamer distinguished between three different ways of experiencing the Thou. The third and highest type of this Thou experience in human relations is to experience the Thou truly as a Thou:

> i.e., not to overlook his claim but to let him really say something to us. Here is where openness belongs. But ultimately this openness does not exist only for the person who speaks; rather anyone who listens is fundamentally open. Without such openness to one another there is no genuine human bond . . . . Openness to the other, then, involves recognising that I myself must accept some things that are against me, even though no one else forces me to do so. (Gadamer, 1992, p. 361)

From this argument, Gadamer (1992) went on to raise the issue of the hermeneutic priority of the question. To be open to the Thou in the way just described—to listen dialogically—requires a certain way of questioning. Gadamer (1992) referred to this questioning as a particular art: it is an art that involves being able to preserve an orientation to openness. To question means to open up, to place in the open. It also meant, for Gadamer, the art of being able to prevent the question from being suppressed by dominant opinions— to prevent premature closure.

In keeping with our development of the idea of dialogue here, we can also suggest that questions need to be asked from genuine curiosity designed to open up the other's talking more and more. Stephen Littlejohn (email correspondence, 30 May 1996) has designed a training exercise based on this notion of listening by questioning. In the exercise, the listening participant is instructed to only ask questions of the other and not to offer comments, personal opinions, and the like. As Littlejohn pointed out, this exercise is very difficult because we are not accustomed to asking questions. We usually want to affirm what the other is saying by linking it to our experiences ("Oh yes, that happened to me too. Did you know, only the other day . . ."); or change the topic to something we are more interested in ("Oh, that reminds me of something else. I was just talking about it with ..."). In other words, we are far more accustomed to holding our own ground than being profoundly open to the other.

When we want to engage in dialogue as a form of practical inquiry into our world, it is the listening-by-questioning mode that is critical. As a practical inquirer, our task is to open up new possibilities in practice by asking questions, not by providing answers. Our task is also to strive for what "we" can co-construct, not what "I" want to say. It is in this striving for what "we" can construct that we create that knowing-from I talked about in the previous section and in chapter 4, and it is in this striving by dialogical listening that we are bent on a form of knowing-from that is at the heart of dialogical inquiry.

Reflections on uncertainty

Time and again, I've explicitly or implicitly said that achieving dialogue is inherently uncertain. It is not a process that can be controlled, only coconstructed, nor is it a process that can be agreed upon in advance and then automatically achieved. Dialogue is not so much a goal as something to strive for collectively. When and if it is achieved, it is most likely to be for the fleeting moment—that moment of mutuality referred to by Carl Rogers in his dialogue with Martin Buber (Cissna & Anderson, 1998).

Nevertheless, it is the striving that counts; it is the hard work in dialogical listening and questioning for the experience of the other. It is also the hard work in standing in the tension between holding your own ground and being profoundly open. This is, yet again, another way of talking about the idea of acting in good faith with participants and the process. Good faith requires a profound openness to the experience of the process and of the other(s) in it.

To finish the discussion here I want to offer a selection of questions developed by Sallyann Roth (1998) for you to reflect upon. I gratefully thank Sallyann Roth for allowing me to use these questions, and apologize if my abridging mars her intent. It is these types of questions that express one way of preparing for dialogical listening. They also show the orientation needed for remaining truly open to the other and the experience. It is these very same questions that could suggest to you how it might be possible for yourself to remain profoundly open in conversation. Imagine what form of practical inquiry could emerge if you took this dialogic orientation in communicating with others. Think of the "I" voice as yourself as you read and reflect.

When I meet people who challenge my views, beliefs, or values:
- *What makes it possible for me to listen to them?*
- *What makes it possible for me to invite them to tell me more about what they think and feel?*
- *What makes it possible for me to ask them how they came to think and feel as they do?*

What kinds of actions and contexts encourage me to:
- *Abandon assumptions that I know what others mean?*
- *Turn my passion to inquiring about things I do not or cannot understand?*
- *Reveal how much I do not understand?*

What do I do that:
- *Calls forth from others something that is unusual for them to speak of openly?*
- *Brings forward responses of unusual complexity and richness?*
- *Calls forward other people's reflections, or their most passionate intentions?*

How can I remember to listen:
- *Fully, openly, with genuine interest, without judgment and without argument,*
- *To another's challenging, or different, ideas, feelings, beliefs?*

How can I stay open:
- *To hearing fresh things even in the other's familiar words?*

What does each of us need to do to gain the vision, the will, the strength, and the simple doggedness to travel this path?

Research practices

In the last chapter, I talked about a particular form of communicating, that of dialoguing. I took dialogue to be an exemplar form of a self-affirming communicating process. I also talked about this process as a form of practical inquiry that requires particular ways of relating with others in our questioning and listening. I ended the last chapter by asking you to imagine what form of practical inquiry could emerge if you took this dialogical orientation in communicating with others. That question raises other ones. How would we be acting/participating in research if we were sensitive to these questions? Is any research possible? What could it be like? What could it accomplish?

Hopefully, it is clear from the preceding six chapters that whatever the research is, it is not the mainstream style of research found in many communication journals—that research is still well-embedded in the assumptions of modernity. Instead, I want to explore here and in the next two chapters a far more involved, practical process of engaging in communicating to understand the very same process. In this exploration I will draw on many of the ideas and concepts introduced earlier. However, here I will employ them to illustrate particular forms of research practice.

The exemplar form of dialoguing is a starting point for a consideration of one form of research practice, although not the only one. As I said in the last chapter, dialogue is not necessarily something we would want to achieve all of the time, nor would it be possible to do so. This is also the case with different research practices. Nevertheless, it is the ideal or vision of dialogue that guides me here and can help orient us to the overriding purpose of these new research practices: to open up new possibilities in practice by asking questions, not providing answers.

ᕙ Research positions

Positionality

One of the first things we have to come to terms with is our position as researchers: where we are standing/being in relation to what we are researching. Here the particular concern is with our position in relation to other persons in communicating. It needs to be emphasised that in this very talk of position, we are simultaneously rejecting any notion of neutrality and acknowledging the reflexive relationship between text and context that I discussed in chapter 2. To explore this notion, I draw on two compatible propositions.

Shotter (1984) proposed the grammatical notion of a person to capture a sense of position. When we give accounts of communicative activity, we can do so from one of three positions: the first (I), second (you), or third (she, he, it) persons. Accounts in the first person are from the position of the actor in the process. Accounts in the second person are addressed to the other actor in the process. Accounts in the third person take the position of observer of both the first and second persons. Each person's position, then, provides a different viewpoint of the action, more or less removed from it.

Sless (1986) similarly argued that the concept of position is critical to our understanding of communicating. Sless was particularly concerned with understanding the visual communication process as reflected in relationships among readers, authors, and texts. He argued that there are two basic positions a person can take in the process, as well as a successive number of removed positions. In any communicative process one is either an author or reader of a text—there is no independent, objective position. However, you could be a reader or author second, third, or more removed. These removed positions occur when, for example, a mass media researcher offers a reading/interpretation of a violent television program that includes a claim that children (as viewers) cannot distinguish between fact and fiction and therefore should not watch such violent programs. In this instance, the researcher is offering a reading (hers or his) of a reading done by children.

Neither Sless or Shotter, however, suggested that there is a direct linear relationship between position and the nature of the account of communication. Instead, both evoked a different, and the same, metaphor—that of landscape. As describers of the human social landscape we can take various positions in that landscape and what we see is dependent on where we are standing: "As the position (s)he occupies changes so does the scene, and as certain views become visible, others disappear" (Sless, 1986, p. 31). The landscape is an elastic one; wherever we stand, we change the shape of the landscape around us.

There is, in fact, no complete landscape—no complete and unalterable view of communicating. Instead, there are an infinite array of understandings of the communicative landscape in which we find ourselves or, more pertinent, project ourselves. It is this notion of position, and its consequences that ultimately denies the possibility of objective knowledge. All inquiries into the nature of communicating are interventions, not neutral observations. In the very act of inquiring into communicating from within the communication landscape, we are intervening in that landscape (Penman, 1988). This intervention is unavoidable, as well as being highly variable.

However, some interventions are better than others. If we are concerned with the practice/experience of communicating, we do not want to adopt a position that occludes that view altogether. Rather, we need to adopt a position as close to the experience of communicating as possible. Essentially, we need to be standing in communicating.

Primary research position

Elsewhere I have called this position—of standing in communicating—the *primary research position* (e.g., Penman, 1995, 1997). I was first inspired to consider this notion by a poignant remark made by a systemic therapist at a conference some years ago. A number of us were participating in a discussion session with one of the keynote speakers, Michael White (1993). The conversation among participants took quite an interesting turn when a cognitive behavior therapist accused (and there is no other word for it) the speaker of having no empirical evidence to support his way of construing therapy. Without a blink of an eyelid, the speaker turned to the cognitive therapist and said that was only a concern for those academics doing secondary research; he was doing primary research.

What an interesting distinction, but what did he mean by it? As the conversation proceeded, I generated this concept of primary research: It was participatory, oriented toward practice and, by implication, change. It was also done within the experience of communicating, not outside of it. For Michael White, psychotherapy was primary research. For my exploration here, I want to develop this same proposition for primary communication research—that it is participatory, oriented toward practice and, by implication, change. In doing so, I fully acknowledge the parallels between doing this form of research and engaging in therapeutic practices—at least of a certain systemic, dynamic form (Penman, 1995)—although perhaps it is necessary to also point out that there are differences, more of emphasis and orientation than of clear divides. In primary research the emphasis is much more strongly on the authorial domain of experience than it is or needs to be in therapeutic practices. Primary researchers have a moral obligation to offer stories/accounts of the experience of communicating in which they are participating.

At this point I need to reintroduce some propositions first introduced in chapter 4, where I considered how we could find our way about in communicating, and do so wisely. There, I suggested that we are always moving between the role of hero in the moral domain—acting into the process—and the role of author in the aesthetic domain—reflecting on/comprehending the process. I also suggested that in the moving-between we are involved in a trueing process (Dewey, 1981); by which truth is located firmly in action (Campbell, 1992). These two domains and the trueing process of moving-between are also the spaces open to researchers in the primary position.

However, when we then go on to consider researching communicating in communicating, we need to take care. The world becomes a little slippery, and our (or at least my) capacity to hold on to where we are, in what, and when, can turn elusive. Some practical examples may help here—even if I am preempting further developments later in the chapter.

Consider a research project on people's conversational practices in particular contexts. In order to understand/explore this from the position of primary research, you need to enter a conversation about their conversations. Here, you are engaged in a real-time movement between the two domains, as you are both acting and authoring as you proceed in the conversation. You are acting in the moral domain as you proceed to engage in the conversation with other(s), being directly accountable to them as you do so. You are also authoring in the aesthetic domain as you generate, out of your conversation, various understandings about their conversational practices.

Alternatively, you might consider another research project in which you wanted to explore the ways in which people understand and use a particular text or document to help them (or not) in their everyday lives. Again you need to enter a conversation about their reading/understanding, and again you are engaged in moving between the domains. In this instance, rather than presume the ways in which the text is read, you are communicating with them about their relationship with the text and the readings that they generate from it.

What makes both of these examples of primary research is that there is a clear recognition that it is in communicating that the research is taking place. The people of the research focus are physically present with you, and you are, by implication, directly accountable to them. There are two different ways in which this accountability gets played out. In the first instance, you are accountable for the understandings you offer them as you proceed in your inquiry in communicating. In the second instance, they can hold you accountable for what you offer and how you proceed in the offering. In other words, by being physically present in communicating with the people of concern, you can be held up to their moral demands.

In the primary research position there is a moral responsibility that simply cannot be ignored (Penman, 1992)—to both the participants in the process and to the process itself. It is the same moral responsibility that I have been discussing in various ways throughout the last three chapters, and which can be best met by acting in good faith. As I hoped I showed in the last chapter, engaging in practices to bring about the possibility of dialogue provides us with morally responsible ways of participating. So primary research is also oriented to a dialogic potential. In the act of participating well in primary research, we are fostering the possibility of dialogue. To do this, we need to bring into play the four characteristics I described in chapter 6—acting authentically, being future orientated, collaborating, and being present—and employ dialogic listening and questioning skills.

Secondary positions

We cannot be in the primary participation position all of the time, and sometimes the circumstances cannot allow it. We adopt a secondary position whenever the source of our research concern is at least one step removed from our direct experience with them, and thus from our direct accountability to them.

Such a secondary position can occur when, for example, we are "reading" a video of a conversation, or someone's written account of an experience. Although there is still an engagement here, the nature of the engagement is different—it is directly with the text, not with the embodied persons and your experience with them. You cannot foster the possibility of dialogue in such engagements. On the other hand, it is still possible to use dialogue in its descriptor role for describing communication practices in particular ways.

I talked about these two different approaches to dialogue in chapter 6, drawing directly on the distinction made by Stewart and Zediker (1999). Using dialogue in its descriptor role requires a sufficiently removed position to be able to see the joint action (Shotter, 1993) and a sufficiently rich vocabulary to elaborate on this joint action in ways that capture the lived experiences between others.

I have no problem with these sort of secondary positions, provided that the researcher explicitly recognizes the limits of such a position (specifically, the limits on understanding others' experiences). However, I do have problems with other secondary research positions in which the researcher is far removed from the realm of experience. Secondary research from a removed (and often far removed) position is the only one possible for a conventional social scientist/researcher. In that form of research the very aim is to distance oneself from the object of study, so as not to contaminate/bias the data. In that form of research the actual lived experience of the person is denied for the sake of objectivity. It is actually ironic that, even though the researcher is often in a primary position with the researched, the experiential component is denied, in order to get to a far removed position, outside of the world of experience. I say more about these ironic consequences later in this chapter.

⟪ Research questions and accomplishments

It may be useful at this point to recall Toulmin's (1990) analysis from chapter 2. There, I described the four moves made by Cartesian rationalists so that they could explore their context-free questions in pursuit of pure truth. They moved from the oral to the written, from the particular case to the universal principle, from the local context to the general abstraction, and from the timely to the timeless. As I noted in that discussion, these four moves are still reflected in the conventional, empirical methods used in some arenas in communication studies today.

What I am trying to do here is, in some way, reverse these four moves, and shift back to the oral, the particular, the local, and the timely. I am not concerned with discovering underlying causes, or explaining why people act/say as they do; nor am I concerned with generalities or abstractions. Engaging in primary communication research requires different research questions and accomplishes different things than does more traditional, secondary (removed) research. Most important, it is concerned with exploring possibilities and enabling practical action from a primary research position.

At this point, it may strike some of you that what I am talking about is a form of action research, particularly the community-based action research advocated by people like Stringer (1996). As Stringer described it, "Community-based action research speaks to the current crisis of research by envisaging a collaborative approach to investigation that seeks to engage 'subjects' as equal and full participants in the research process" (1996, p. 9). There is no doubt my arguments here speak to the same crisis and envisaging. I also agree with the focus of action research: "Community-based action research provides a model for enacting local, action-oriented approaches to inquiry, applying small scale theorising to specific problems in specific situations (Stringer, 1996, p. 9). However, I cannot unequivocally agree with one of the fundamental premises that Stringer claimed drives community-based action research— the search for the community problem. Although I have more to say against this problem-orientation in the next two chapters, suffice it to say here that a concentrated exploration of the problem is not always necessary, or desirable, in order to generate new possibilities for action. Indeed, it can well be the case that a zealous search for the problem mitigates against a dialogic potential. It is certainly the case that such a search almost inevitably leads you to face into the past with a backward orientation—an orientation counter to the forward one required in setting up conditions for dialogue.

I also want to be cautious about having my arguments equated with other forms of action research, especially those that arose in the heady, radical days of the 1960s; characterized primarily by a focus on direct political action and an eschewing of any theory or research interests. Observers at the time (e.g., Rappaport, 1970) lamented the fact that action researchers had come to subordinate research and knowledge aims to action interests: a position in direct contradiction to the original proposals for action research. For example, in Kurt Lewin's arguments for action science, he claimed that "[t]here is nothing as practical as a good theory" (1951, p. 169). I share this sentiment. Although I am concerned with action here, I am not rejecting conceptual or research interests. Indeed, If you recall the arguments in chapter 3, I am very much in favor of the development of practical theory—theory that allows us to go on in our lived experiences, and to go on well.

There is a third element that distinguishes my proposals here from other forms of action research—my orientation to communicating as the central focus. Although there is no doubt that many recent action research approaches emphasize the importance of communication in the collaborative action research process, the communicative assumptions are those still firmly based in a tradition of modernity. For example, Stringer (1996) and Jacobson and Kolluri (1999) drew directly on Habermas to propose four fundamental conditions that need to be met if communication is to be effective—understanding, truth, sincerity and appropriateness. For me, the communication process is far more complex than this implies, and the conditions for good communicating are far different (see chapters 5 & 6).

So, yes, I am proposing a form of action research, but not one directly equivalent with other earlier or contemporary forms. The social constructionist assumptions on which this whole book rests leads us to a different notion of action and change than those contemplated in other action research arenas. However, let us now have a closer look at the form of research practices I am advocating. This is most easily dealt with by way of looking at the questions asked in, and of, the process, and the accomplishments brought about in it.

With what questions?

Just as every question we ask of others implicates the answer we get, the research question we set ourselves generates, in the end, its own answers. Equally as important, the type of question we ask implicates a particular method. However, asking questions that are appropriate to the circumstances of primary research can sometimes be very hard indeed. The past 3 centuries of modernity have not only inculcated us with a particular way of valuing things and doing things, but also with a particular way of asking about certain things and not others, and asking in certain ways and not others. As an example, let's consider the articles in a 1997 issue of the *Journal of Communication* (vol. 47, no. 3). The questions posed by the five research articles were:

- How can we "expand the study of advertising and examine it as a means of communication that is something more than capitalist propaganda?" (Tinic, 1997, p. 4).
- "How [do] news frames in campaign coverage affect individual's interpretation of campaigns?" (Rhee, 1997, p. 26).
- "What forms of deviance account for much of the variation in decisions about crime news?" (Pritchard & Hughes, 1997, p. 49).
- What industrial, commercial, and social factors influence the visual images in textbooks? (Perlmutter, 1997, p. 68)
- What is the relationship among earthquake severity, media coverage, and private/ government aid? (Simon, 1997, p. 82).

These are seemingly normal questions. We find them all the time in our research journals. However, they are not questions appropriate to primary research. First, every one of these questions is being asked from a removed position. For example, in the first article, Tinic (1997) offered us a reading of a Benneton advertising campaign that drew on advertising images, and public announcements by the company and media and other groups criticizing the campaign. In drawing on the latter, Tinic was in fact doing a reading of a reading, from a removed position. In the second article, Rhee (1997) employed a field experimental design in which participants were asked six preformulated questions about the manipulated information material and then were required to write a letter about it. In both instances, the answers to the preformulated questions and the narrative propositions were rendered into numerical measures, thus once again removing the researcher well away from the primary understanding experience.

The questions asked by the authors of the five articles just cited are also not appropriate to primary research, because every one of them is addressed to an abstract noun (advertising, news frames, deviance factors, etc.), presumably doing the "thing." Where, I wonder, are the people in the process? This is particularly pertinent in the fifth article (Simon, 1997), in which four objective measures were taken—of earthquake severity, media coverage, private contributions and government assistance—to show various correlations between them. There were no people at all, just abstract phenomena.

Just as important, all of the questions raised in the five articles require generalized, abstract answers that presume some notion of cause and effect, or at least of influence. Indeed, three of the five papers explicitly mention this:

- "Generalised principles about news and US justice systems can emerge from the accumulation of theoretically focused case studies" (Pritchard & Hughes, 1997, p. 65).
- "Narrative data generated in an experimental setting can provide valid evidence about the outcome of interpretation" (Rhee, 1997, p. 45).
- "Provides strong evidence of the media's causal role in shaping the public's prosocial behaviours in response to real world events" (Simon, 1997, p. 92).

There are many problems with questions that lead to these sort of answers, but two are pertinent here. First, I have an immense distrust of the answers, even when treated specifically, because in none of the papers is the voice of experience expressed. The measures of people's experiences, beliefs, or whatever, have all been indirectly inferred. This was particularly the case in the research described by Rhee (1997), who had the opportunity to talk with people about their experiences but still converted them into numerical data.

My second problem is that I don't know what to do with the answers. I realize that this is not usually a research concern. It is usually sufficient to describe and justify the findings and just leave it at that. But again, that is an outcome of the more removed research against which I am arguing. With primary research, the concern is far different. At the beginning of chapter 6, I said that once we recognize the materiality of communicating, we are able to directly face the practical concerns of our world and ask, from the position of participation, what we can do. This is the basic question I am concerned with here: I want to know what positive, specific actions for the good of others I can take from any research understandings. If there is, for example, a correlation between media coverage and private charitable organizations, what can I do with this (especially recognizing the nature of correlational data)? Additionally, what could I want to do?

On occasions when I have made similar arguments to those put forth here, I have been challenged with questions like "Well how would you research the effects of the media?" My answer is, "I wouldn't!" It is the wrong type of question altogether for my way of primary research and practical action, although this is not to say that you cannot ask questions about media from a primary research position. The difference is you need to ask the questions of the people interacting with the media and those questions need to be about their inter-active experience in particular contexts. This approach has been taken on board over the past decade or so in a number of different media-experience research projects (e.g., Turnbull, 1998).

So how can we ask questions that don't lead in the directions of which I have just been critical? The questions need to be context specific, be oriented directly to experience, and recognise the historicity of our asking and answer-ing. A common form of questioning that I use in thinking about any particular communication research context is this:

- Who are the participants in the process—current ones, ones who should/could be involved, or ones deliberately excluded?
- What do/could each of the participants want from/in the process that would be good for them?
- How do they want this? What communicative practices are best for them?
- What type of judgments need to be made to know that the practices are good or best for them?

In my own research practices, I have found these questions to be important guides when considering how to approach issues relating to media, albeit media of a very different sort than popularly studied. In this instance, I am referring to public documents. One particularly significant project had to do with how people understand government legislation, using specific examples of legislation pertaining to child care and elder care. If we focus just on the elder care legislation, the major participants in the process include the elderly person in receipt of care, any family caregivers, the persons running elder care/nursing homes, the administrators of the legislation, and those who process care claims. What each of the participants need from the process of interacting with the legislation is to understand what they are allowed to do or not to do, what they can claim for, and how they can actually do it in the most beneficial/efficient way. As you could imagine, the current legislation did not meet their needs of understanding. After extensive conversations with the different types of participants it became apparent that their understanding needs required a radically different legislative structure; along, of course, with more easily understood expressions of legal concepts. Two key themes emerged: the need for a narrative structure, and the need to write to enable action. In subsequent developments of possibilities and working collabor-atively with participants, it also became apparent that the more the writing style and structure emulated conversational features the more readily it was understood (see Penman, 1993).

The form of questions I use lead us to inquire into people's experiences and understandings in particular local contexts. They are of a different order entirely from the common form of questions found in many research journals, and they obviously lead to a different form of answer. In asking these inquiring questions, we can generate data that show the rich variability of experience; whereas the conventional style of questions produces answers in an aggregated data form, in which the people are far removed from the data—if they were ever there in the first place. Many researchers seem to have shied away from this rich variability in favor of aggregates, because aggregates appear easier to deal with —there is a need for only the one answer or solution. However, there is a critical moral import in this use of aggregates. In chapter 4 I discussed Bauman's (1991) account of how social organization is able to neutralize the impact of moral action through three complementary arrangements. One of these arrangements requires that human beings and their individual actions are turned into a collection of different attributes or traits in aggregate form. Thus, the moral import of action falls on no person at all. This is the end consequence of asking questions from removed positions of abstract nouns which bring about aggregated answers.

What accomplishments?

If we asks questions in the way I am talking about, we are not interested in theory development, per se. We are particularly not interested in the form of abstract theory reflected in much of contemporary research. John Shotter (e.g., 1997a & 1997b) argued against this "way of theory" and for a "social poetic" instead, drawing significantly from the work of Wittgenstein. As he pointedly put it: Theory is after the fact, beside the point, and renders the unique event invisible (1998b). By way of contrast, primary research is concerned with the events as they are unfolding—with the consequences, not the antecedents, to use Dewey's (1981) phrase. Primary research is concerned with the point of practice, not with inferences and generalities about it. Primary research is also concerned with the unique event—the local, the particular, and the timely that I mentioned earlier.

In primary research we are fundamentally concerned with the experienced reality that is jointly co-constructed. It is only in primary research that we can genuinely understand the act of communicating; that we realise we are involved as persons in the construction of a mutual social reality, not as objective observers of someone else's; that we recognise the real reflexivity in our position as researchers of the process we are always in. Most important, it is only primary research that allows us to deal with primary "data"—real, empirical data in the real, communicating world.

When Barnett Pearce commented on an earlier version of this argument, he related a very pertinent comment of Vern Cronen's regarding empirical data that I would like to use here. According to Cronen, empirical data has undergone an ironic shift. It is now taken to mean such things as marks on a questionnaire that stand for something, such as attitudes, that are in people's heads. However, these attitudes are only inferred, not observed, and hence are not strictly empirical. What is perhaps equally as ironic about this shift is that the social scientist has to take the utterances of the interviewee (the primary experience) and convert them into categories and numbers that then stand for the experience. We can describe this ironic shift as going from experiencing (active verb form) to cognition (noun form).

Using interviews to generate questionnaire data is a very typical example of the removed, secondary research position I mentioned earlier in this chapter. Taking this as an example, we can actually see that there a number of other ironic shifts that have to take place to go from the primary to the removed, secondary position. A second shift occurs when we move the notion of the independent variable from we-who-act-into-a-situation to something that we manipulate and then observe. In the interview example just mentioned, it is the interviewer doing the manipulation with the interview schedule in order to record the response observations. In this second ironic shift, the interviewer has moved from participating to observation.

Third, there is the shift from the dialogical (using the term in the descriptive sense described in chapter 6) to the monological. Although the conversation that generated the questionnaire data was between two people, and in that sense dialogical, the interviewer has to deny the engagement and generate a semblance of monological reality. The very training that good interviewers (of that old style) are subject to makes them monological—in order to avoid contamination of the so-called observations. This is particularly apparent in those oft occurring interview situations in which the interviewee expresses confusion or puzzlement about the question and all the interviewer is allowed to do is to repeat the same puzzling question.

Fourth, there is a shift from mutual constructing to closed preconstruction.

Despite the claim of conventional social scientists that they are trying to discover a truth or a reality, the very nature of the so-called discovery process closes of all but the narrowest of pathways. In our example, every question on the questionnaire closes off anything but the answer in the form required—typically, yes/no or agree/disagree. The conversation has been preconstructed by the person developing the questionnaire schedule. The impelling force of this preconstruction is reflected in the monosyllablic replies typical of many interview situations.

Finally, in removed, secondary communication research (of which there is far too much), communication scholars engage in the most ironic shift of all. In order to account for the process of communication, they use communication experiences—whether it be from interactions with others or with written material—from a dialogical reality, and twist it into monological, cognitive data, in order to be able to explain communication (noun form).

When all of the shifts are pointed out, it becomes obvious how removed this type of secondary research is from empirical reality, as well as its inadequacies to deal with real, practical problems in the communicating world. What concerns us then, in doing primary research, is generating under-standings and possibilities in and out of empirical realities. It is these under-standings that, if generated well, offer new possibilities for going forward, in that particular context.

The real accomplishment of primary research, then, is practical: it is both about practice and helps to brings about new practice. I have more to say about these practical accomplishments in the last chapter. But a remark by Stringer (1996), in talking about the difference between traditional and community-based action research, poignantly captures the importance of the practical: "A colleague approached me after listening to my report on one of the action research projects in which I had been involved. 'You know,' she said, 'the difference with your work is that you expect something to actually happen as a result of your activities'." (Stringer, 1996, p. 11).

⟪ Research judgments

When we enter the research domain I am describing here, the conventional means for making judgments are discarded. We cannot draw on notions of validity or reliability; and we cannot resort to statistical inferences and say that something is significant simply because it fell below a probability level of 0.5. Most important, we are unable to prove that something is true. The domain in which we are moving cannot accommodate the common-sense or correspondence notion of truth—that a statement is true if it conforms with the facts or agrees with reality. In the research domain described here, there is no independent reality to agree with and there are no facts to be had. In this domain, all judgments are made from within the process, not from without.

So what alternative claims can we make about our research? How can we know we have done it well? I suggest at least two related criteria: the quality of the process, and the quality of the accomplishments. To deal with quality, I want to return to Campbell's notion of truth: "The truth, therefore, is not to be found by renouncing our historicity, nor in trying to construct an impersonal and timeless account of reality which flies in the face of our own humanity. It is rather to be achieved in the quality and authenticity of our faithful life-activities" (Campbell, 1992, p. 438).

In other words, we are engaged in quality primary research when we, as researchers, act authentically and faithfully in the process. How do we do this? We enact the features of conversation that are likely to enhance the possibility of dialogue. We engage in the process, acting authentically into the conversational moment. We are future orientated, going with the flow of the participants' conversations. We collaborate with the participants, working mutually on the development of the methods by which new understandings and changes are brought about. We are embodied persons with our participants, orientated to experience. Most important, we use the dialogic listening by questioning mode I described in chapter 6, striving to achieve the form of knowing-from that it is at the heart of dialogical inquiry.

But still I can hear people ask how can we really know we've done it well. Perhaps the best answer of all is to ask the other participants in the process. For me, that is the ultimate test, as it were, and I find there is nothing more rewarding than have participants say things like "I never really expected it to be like this. I really enjoyed it." I appreciate that such a criteria for making judgments would simply be laughed at (if not worse) by mainstream researchers. Nevertheless, it is a perfectly legitimate one within the domain of primary research and within the language game I am working in here. We can only know from within our communicating experience and this includes the other participants' offerings of their experience to you, the researcher.

If the process works well, the accomplishments will also be good ones, in the sense of opening up new possibilities and of enabling further action (as I mentioned in chapter 4). If we can demonstrate that we have done this, then we can truly claim a good research process. Usually this demonstration is done via an evaluation process. I made reference to an element of this evaluation process in the previous section on questions. There, one of the primary research questions posed was "What type of judgments need to be made to know that the practices are good or best for the participants?"

In the example of the legislative project I used to illustrate a way of posing research questions, the judgments centred around the participants' capacity to read, understand and use the legislation in a way beneficial to them. In order to properly make such a judgment, new legislation had to be written using the guidelines developed. Participants were then asked what they wanted to know about the legislation that was important to them, and to use the new version to find the answers. They were able to do so and they could understand what it was they could do. In this instance, then, the accomplishment was positive and the research process a success.

Other types of projects call for different forms of evaluation. Stringer (1996), for example, relied on a "Fourth Generation Evaluation" process for judging the success of his community-based action research. This form of evaluation is carried out as a joint construction by stakeholder groups who describe the accomplishments from their point of view and identify those that are successful and others that require further action. In other words, the accomplishments are judged in terms of their acceptability to the participants involved in the research process.

Whatever form of evaluation is used, the critical point is that the accomplishments are judged from the point of view of the participants in the research process, not solely that of the researcher. This reaffirms the whole point of conducting primary research: to bring about practical change for the purposes of the participants. It is also congruent with an important feature of practical theory discussed in chapter 2. Practical theory, according to Cronen (1995a), must be assessed in terms of its consequences, specifically in terms of how it makes human life better. Primary research must be assessed similarly— in terms of how it makes human life better.

8

Research tools

In chapter 7 we looked at a notion of primary research that is participatory, oriented towards practice and, by implication, change. This form of research leads us to ask entirely different questions, with different accomplishments and different means of judgment, than does mainstream contemporary research. In order to practice this form of research, we need to be oriented to achieving dialogic potential by engaging authentically, collaborating mutually, orienting to the future, and being physically present with the others.

However, this still doesn't get us to the nitty gritty of doing it. What exactly can/should we be doing in the practice of primary research? If we were using conventional methods, we could turn to a social research methods book to tell us exactly how to design and run an experiment, how to draw samples for surveys, how to construct questionnaires, and so on. But we are not using conventional methods, so what other methods are relevant here?

First of all I think it would help if we stepped away from the word *methods* for a moment, to avoid the conventional implications of such a words (e.g., formal, precise, orderly, controlled). Instead, I want to use the idea of a set of research tools. I am drawing on John Shotter's (1993) work here when I use the notion of research tools. The tools in our toolbox are our ways of understanding.

Each tool not only helps us see and make connections, but can also help others find other uses we did not see. So, what I am asking in this chapter is what notions, ways of understanding, metaphors, or other concepts can be useful for helping us make connections and offer possibilities? What tools can we use for sensemaking?

It is the range and variety of tools in this toolbox that distinguish a good participant researcher from other participants in the process. This is our special offering in the process, but it is not an offering of theory. There is, as John Shotter (1993) wrote, no necessary or logical order to the tools in the tool-box. Indeed, Shotter often finds the tools are hardly ever in the box, but instead are spread everywhere and often not accessible. I also find that this is the case. However, in writing here I am reassembling them again and, being an orderly person, I find it useful to put tools for different uses in different places. Note, however, that this ordering is not one of logical necessity, but of practical convenience.

Although, as I've just said, there is no necessary order in the toolbox, it may be useful to make a convenient distinction among three different sets of tools: a set for preparing for research, a set for participating in the research, and a set for telling of the practice. But, as with all ordering processes, this is neither complete nor are the categories mutually exclusive. Indeed, there is considerable overlap among the three sets.

✍ Preparatory tools

In an analysis of a conversation between Buber and Rogers, Cissna and Anderson (1998) pointed to five principles on which Buber and Rogers agreed. One of these was "[t]hat the therapist is the more active participant who creates the conditions for the relationship and, thus, for dialogic potential" (p. 70). In exactly the same way, it is the researcher doing primary research who is responsible for creating the conditions for the researcher–participator relationship. The preparations made for the research practice are critical to establishing the potential for dialogical inquiry.

Setting the scene

Once we have decided what we want to explore with participants, following the approach to questions I discussed in the last chapter, we then need to consider the local and timely context in which talk can proceed and take on meaning. Where and when we talk and with whom becomes one of the many contextual factors that contribute to meaning generation; as do how we introduce our talk to participants and set the ground rules for proceeding.

Deciding on participants will be a function of the research questions we are asking. But, with this form of primary research, we must bear in mind that we need to be able to physically participate with all of them. We also need to remember that because we are only concerned with the local and particular, we are not choosing people because they are representative or typical. Instead, we are selecting people because they are relevant.

In community-based action and other practical research projects, these relevant participants are commonly referred to as *stakeholders*. I confess to finding this a somewhat unfortunate metaphoric use. Traditionally, a stake-holder was the person who held the money for other people making bets (stakes) on an event. Now, it has come to mean "having an investment in." Note, however, that the root metaphor is still an economic one. For my purposes, I prefer simply to talk about participants, or perhaps research collaborators. In choosing these participants, we are asking the first of the general primary research questions discussed in the last chapter: Who are the participants in the process—current ones, who could/should be involved, or ones deliberately excluded?

Not only is it important to choose relevant people, we also should try to choose those with the potential to show a broad range of differences in experience. The narrower the range of difference is, the narrower the opening for new possibilities to emerge. I'm reminded of the importance of this selection process in one project where I was concerned with understanding how various people in an organization saw internal communication practices. Previous research (done by others in the organization) had shown that they had serious communication problems. But, on reviewing that research, I noted that only staff to a certain level had been part of the research—no management levels were included. So this view of communication problems was only that held by a segment of the organisation and we really didn't know the picture from all different positions.

The second decision to be made is where and when the research will be conducted. This, in part, is dependent on whom you will be inviting. You need to consider where and when will it be most convenient or comfortable to the participants. Clearly, if you are conducting research into issues to do with, say, working mothers, it is not convenient to schedule meetings during their working hours or at places that are hard for them to get to out of working hours. It may be that you need to talk with them in their workplace or at child care facilities instead.

You also need to consider whether a familiar or neutral setting is more appropriate. By *appropriate*, I mean appropriate for setting up a dialogue potential, while showing respect to the participants. For example, if you are doing research into organizational communication practices, you usually have to work with participants in their familiar work setting. However, it is best if meetings do not take place where participants are easily found or distracted.

Once you have decided on the range of participants and when/where the research inquiry is to take place, you need to approach potential participants. How you introduce the research is critical at this point. The way you talk about the project and what you say provides the initial framework within which understanding proceeds. You must consider how to explain what you are interested in, remembering the need for good faith while so doing. You also should consider how you describe what you want of the other participants, and what you can hope to achieve.

In the organizational communication project I mentioned earlier, I was most concerned that the initial understanding framework was a positive one. The organization was very good at problem identification and general blaming, and from the beginning, it was crucial that I turn this around. It was also important that participants heard my words, not those of organizational people involved in the project. Here is a version of the fax I sent to selected managers at the beginning of the project:

> Thank you for agreeing to meet with me at 10.00 a.m. next Friday. As Peter Smith has explained, we are about to enter into the next phase of the cultural intervention strategy to improve internal communication. We believe it is vital that any plans for improvements arise from the active participation of the people concerned.
>
> We are proposing to investigate practical action possibilities with a number of management and staff in Sydney, through the use of structured inquiry and planning sessions and interviews. But before we finalize the structure for these sessions, we wanted to develop an appreciation of the particular context of the Sydney operations. To do this we have requested some time with you and other staff to explore possible issues and help make practical arrangements. In

particular we are concerned to:
- *talk personally with you about our plans and hopes for this next stage*
- *seek your advice on the best ways of setting up the next steps that will fit with other work practicalities*
- *understand any special considerations that we need to take into account*
- *understand the current views on the cultural intervention project to date*
- *consider ways in which we can generate support for our next steps*
- *explore what you think are some of the positive things that can happen from these next steps.*

Over the years of undertaking primary research I have become increasingly aware of the importance of this initial framing. This was reinforced by some early mistakes that arose when I simply relied on others to solicit the support of participants. In so doing, I found myself in conversations with participants that were clearly based on presumptions and expectations totally different from mine. This does not make for a good collaborative process.

The Public Conversation Project in Boston (Becker, Chasin, Chasin, Herzig, & Roth, 1995) also found this type of scene-setting work critical to their work, and have developed a thorough process to ensure that participants enter the process fully informed and committed. Their conversation project is concerned with taking people involved in divisive public debate and creating an opportunity for the possibility of dialogue. Before any of the participants in their dialogic process meet, they are sent a letter and then have a follow-up phone call. These processes help potential participants understand that they are required to engage in a different form of conversation, not a debate. The processes are also designed to bring about agreement based on an understanding of the ground rules for participation. Such scene-setting activity continues into the very time and place of meeting, where all participants are seated in a circular arrangement and the placement of participants is determined in advance.

The advance, scene-setting work done by the members of the Public Conversation Project is carefully designed to encourage dialogue and avoid confrontational debate. Although Public Conversation Project members are not engaged in the precise form of primary research I am talking about here, the scene-setting tools they use are still valuable. These tools highlight such considerations as: ensuring that potential participants genuinely understand what is required, getting agreement in advance on procedural rules, and guaranteeing a neutrality of setting to all participants. In other projects, particularly for research of less controversial topics, not all of these factors may be as important. Nevertheless, the setting must still be carefully prepared in advance.

Rehearsing and anticipating

Usually, in research, we have specific topics or lines of inquiry to explore. However, there are a multitude of ways in which this can be done. As part of the researcher's contribution to creating the conditions for the relationship, we need to rehearse and anticipate conversational directions and possibilities. We particularly need to anticipate possible questions and their implications. Following are two different sets of questions about questions. I use the first set to show how these questions can be used to rehearse and anticipate, giving examples from a research project concerned with understanding how to enhance the counseling role of pharmacists. Here is the first set:

> **If I ask this, what responses are possible?**
> Consider the possible responses from "Do you offer much counseling to patients getting prescriptions filled?" compared with "How do you usually help people with information about the drugs they are taking?"

> **What could these responses mean?**
> "Do you offer much counseling?" could generate responses like "no" or "it depends" which don't get us very far.

> **How could they help us understand and explore new possibilities?**
> "How do you usually help?" tells us far more about practical steps and offers ways of exploring whether they could do it even better.

> **How much do they close off?**
> "Would you like to attend evening drug information sessions?" closes off far more than "Can you think of ways that drug companies might be able to help you in your counseling role?"

> **How could I ask it differently?**
> Rather than asking "Can you think of ways that drug companies?"

*you might get at better practice by asking "Have you found any
information supplied by drug companies particularly helpful for you
in your counseling role?"*

What might be a good outcome of questioning?
*In this instance a good outcome of the questioning is a practical
understanding of how pharmacists counsel, in what contexts, with
whom, and what they find will help them the most in this counselling
practice.*

Here is a second set of questions about questions we could use, developed
by Sallyann Roth (1997) for therapeutic conversations, but just as relevant for
research ones:

**Is this a genuine question? Is it a question to which I don't know
the answer?**
*Only the researcher can answer this, but the point of this question
about the question is that only genuine questions, asked with
curiosity, open up new possibilities.*

**What work do I want this question to do? What will the question
invite?**
*In other words, what answers will this question open up, or prompt
people to give?*

**Is this question more likely to call forth a familiar response or
invite fresh thinking/feeling?**
*Will you just get a response that people have worked out previously,
or will the question make them reassess?*

Is this question likely to call cultural givens into question?
Will the question invite people to think about assumptions?

Is this question likely to generate imagination, creative action?
Will the question open up new possibilities for action?

**Is this question likely to be heard as one that comes from a collab-
orative stance with the other(s)?**
*Will the question make a contribution to the joint development of
sensemaking (described in chapter 6 on dialogue).*

These types of questions help us rehearse conversational possibilities and
assemble useful participatory tools. Indeed, the questions we refine as we
rehearse inevitably end up as part of our participatory tool kit.

⟪⟫ Doing it—tools of the moral hero

This heading was irresistible to me. It conjures up images of the primary researcher entering the research domain bristling with metaphysical tools for use in unknown territory. I am, of course, drawing on Bakhtin's notion of the hero that I introduced in chapter 4 (Bakhtin, 1990; Morson & Emerson, 1989). As primary researchers, we are in the process of participating. We are in the lived experience as Bakhtin's hero and, as such, are acting directly in the moral domain. There are a number of tools on which the primary researcher can draw; all oriented to a dialogic potential and most relying on dialogic listening.

I talked about this notion of dialogic listening in chapter 6, and noted that one of the things that helps us listen dialogically is questioning, albeit questioning in a particular way. This is a form of questioning that preserves an orientation to openness and prevents premature closure, and involves genuine curiosity that opens up the other's talking more and more.

Questions of practice

In our inquiry as primary researchers, our orientation is to the participants' experiences and their practices, not to their preferences, reasonings, or speculation. This is in marked contrast to the survey questions generated by conventional social scientists. Their questions are usually oriented to what presumably goes on in people's heads—what their attitudes, beliefs and opinions are. These are the intramental concepts that I eschewed in chapter 3 and further dismissed in chapter 4.

In chapter 3, I also talked about the necessity of recovering experience, if we are to be concerned with communicating. For Dewey (1981), it was not what we think or feel retrospectively, but what happens in the doings of our living that counts—hence his emphasis on the lived experience. Dewey's arguments return us to the practical everyday realm of acting in communicating—of participating in our social life. Dewey provided good reason for being concerned with the mundane and the ordinary, the minutiae of our everyday experiences. He urged us to ask "What do we experience about things we do and happenings in our world?" This point of experience is our empirical reality and that is the foundation for his philosophic method. I too urge you to ask of your research participants "What do you experience in your everyday world?"

Questions of experience often rely on the use of how and what, but usually not why. Asking "why?" calls for a logical reconstruction, not an experiential account. Questions of practice can be along these lines:

- *How did you experience that television program? What did it mean for you?*
- *How do you understand this? How else could you understand it?*
- *How do you use it in your everyday life? How can it help you?*
- *What was it that struck you the most about that advertisement? How is that so?*
- *What did you hear her say? How could it have been interpreted differently?*

Following is a set of questions we prepared for talking with pharmacists about their counseling role—the project I also used in discussing tools of anticipation and rehearsal. However, keep in mind, that these questions were never intended to be just read as written; they are prompts more than precise questions.

- *What are the main types of things that customers want to know?*
- *How do you usually help customers with this information?*
- *Do you ever give customers information to take away and read later?*
- *Could you help them more? How? What stops you now?*
- *Are there any information materials or sources that you find particularly useful? How are they useful?*
- *Are there any information materials that are not very useful/ never used? In what way aren't they useful?*
- *What is missing from the current range of information materials available to you?*
- *Is there something that you would find particularly useful in helping in your counseling role?*

When using question prompts of this sort, it is not even necessary to follow the sequence given. The critical thing is to follow the flow of the conversation, using the questions as the means to go forward. Nevertheless, in preparing the questions of practice, it is still valuable to consider a possible sequence. The sequence should employ the normal patterns of conversation that allow one question to build on another. It also needs a basic narrative flow, which will help the participants unfold their story. In the example given here, we were concerned to generate a narrative that focused increasingly on the value in use of different types of information materials.

Questions to go forward with

The idea and arguments associated with the notion of appreciative inquiry offer a great deal of possibilities as part of our hero's toolbox (e.g., Cooperrider & Srivastva, 1987; Hammond & Royal, 1998). Appreciative inquiry was developed as a challenge to the traditional problem-solving approach in organizational change processes, geared to identifying the problem and analyzing causes so that the organization can do "less of something [they] do not do well" (Hammond, 1996, p. 23). In contrast, appreciative inquiry is oriented to what an organization does well and doing more of what works (Hammond, 1996). It is partly because of the persuasiveness and utility of this approach and partly because of further arguments in the next chapter that I veer away from the problem-solving orientation of action research such as Stringer's (1996) that I discussed in the last chapter.

Pearce and Littlejohn (1997) identified five major principles that are at the heart of appreciative inquiry, three of which are particularly pertinent here. First, the appreciative inquirer takes a stance of awe and wonder. They are truly curious about how people do things and how things might go better. When I was talking in chapter 6 about dialogue as practical inquiry, I also noted the importance of this research curiosity. We listen dialogically when we are asking questions from true (good faith) curiosity that is designed to open up the other's talking.

It is really important to emphasize here that there is no point in asking questions that simply seem curious; they must be genuinely from the heart. This was the point that Roth (1997) made in her list of questions about questions: "Is this a genuine question? Is it a question to which I don't know the answer?" To be able to ask these questions genuinely provides a real challenge to the primary researcher using appreciative inquiry.

While I was writing this chapter, I was actually engaged in a major appreciative inquiry on organizational communication practices. In planning for the first inquiry session, I spent some time reflecting on things that I was genuinely curious about and really wanted to know. As I reflected, I was struck by (another tool to be discussed in the next section) the amount of change the organization had experienced and how well they holding up in the circumstances. So I became quite curious about how they had managed to do this, and went prepared with questions like these:

- *I've been really impressed with the way you've managed all the changes over the past 12 months. How have you done it so well?*
- *That seems fantastic, are there other things you also do well?*
- *What sort of communication activities or events have helped you do this so well?*

Second, appreciative inquirers avoid problem-talk; they want to look forward to future possibilities, not backward to problems. Problem-talk gets people bogged down in an analysis of the causes of the problems. When we are dealing with communication problems this is inevitable. Although those in a particular communicative context may feel uneasy about the nature of the communication practices, it is not possible to try and find the definitive source of unease, or nature of the problem. Instead, appreciative inquirers want to focus on those things that people do well and explore how they might be able to do more of them. In the organizational example I mentioned earlier, I prepared a number of appreciative questions for the organizational members to use in interviewing each other. Some of these questions were:

- *Can you think of a time when you felt really appreciated for the work you had done? Could you describe this time? Who was involved? What was it about? What allowed it to happen? What circumstances helped? What made it a good time for you?*

- *Can you think of a time when you really listened to and understood someone else? Could you describe this time? Who was involved? What was it about? What allowed it to happen? What circumstances helped? What made it a good time for you?*

Third, appreciative inquirers are forward orientated. They appreciate the positive in participants' contributions, and explore ways in which these can help participants move forward. In this exploration, open questions are asked about possible futures. This forward, open orientation to questions is very much in line with Dewey's (1981) arguments: It is not the antecedent phenomena nor the precedents that are critical to our understandings, but instead the consequent phenomena and the possibilities for future action. This forward orientation is also one of the four requirements for establishing a dialogic potential. Again, drawing on my organizational example, we could ask questions like:

- *What would you need to do to make sure that this happens more often? What other things would you need to do to implement these practices?*
- *What can you do to bring this possibility about?*
- *How else could you do this even better?*

Other questions of engagement

There are a multitude of ways in which we can engage with others by questioning; including our questions of practice and appreciation described earlier. Some further question tool sets were described by Pearce and Littlejohn (1997) in their discussion of model projects in "transcendent discourse." For them, this form of discourse displays an eloquence that can take people beyond, or outside, the character of their normal moral disputes. Transcendent discourse has five general characteristics: it is philosophical, comparative, dialogic, critical, and transformative.

Pearce and Littlejohn (1997) discuss three model projects in transcendent discourse that used a number of useful participatory tools. For example, in describing the National Issues Forum project, they offered a list of sample questions for deliberating a topic and a list of sample question for harvesting values, opinions, and differences. These question sets be could invaluable in any primary research project requiring an exploration of how people understand issues of public importance. Another example was provided in Pearce and Littlejohn's (1997) description of the Public Conversation Project, a project I talked about earlier when describing some preparatory tools. This project also uses a number of participatory tools. In particular, the Public Conversation Project has a set of proscribed ground rules for conducting conversations designed to be dialogic. These ground rules offer a tool set for managing and guiding the process of communicating. Finally, Pearce and Littlejohn (1997) offered different sets of tools from their Public Dialogue Consortium. Aside from appreciative inquiry (which we have already discussed), they offered a sample set of systemic questions designed to reveal the grammar (from the Co-ordinated Management of Meaning theory; Pearce & Cronen, 1980) of the participants, to challenge that grammar, and to imagine possible futures. They also wrote about the tool of reflecting, in which the interviewer reflects possible connections, contexts, and futures based on answers to systemic and appreciative questions.

There are, of course, other examples and possible sources of yet more participatory tools (e.g., see Stringer, 1996). But the point is that these tool sets are open-ended. I have only described the ones I have found most useful in the contexts in which I have worked. Each different research setting into which we move is likely to call for its own unique set of tools. In part, we have to find them scattered about and, in part, we have to create them, often from the mutually collaborative inquiry process in which we engage.

ᐊᐸ Telling of—tools of the author

In chapter 4, I talked about the aesthetic realm of the author, drawing on both Bakhtin (e.g., Bakhtin, 1990; Morson & Emerson, 1989) and Dewey (1981). In this realm the author takes a stance of looking at the whole and of being able to comprehend a pattern, at least for the moment. In this stance, there is momentary comprehension before the process proceeds again. When we turn our attention to tools of the author, we are talking about tools that can be used to make offerings back into the process of participating, as well as tools that can be used to make offerings of understandings to others outside the primary research process. But regardless of to whom the offerings are made, they are offerings that should tell of something—at least within the language game of the argument discussed here.

This phrase, "telling of", is from John Shotter (1997c) who used it to make a distinction with "telling about." Shotter maintained that we, as academics, have two distinct styles of speaking and writing with which we relate to people around us. There is the professional style that is variously objective, realistic, formal, or neutral which many academics use to present findings, facts, and theories. This is the style in which most conference presentations are still made and most journal articles written. It is a style that tells others about something, as if from afar. In contrast, there is a conversational style, which is more informal: It is "an open, responsive form of talk in which new 'spaces' may be opened up, and others closed, freely, moment by moment" (Shotter, 1997c, p. 8). This is a style that talks from within our involvement with others, and tells of our experiences and our apprehensions. It is this style of telling of that I am concerned with here.

Tools from Wittgenstein

I am drawing heavily on the writings of John Shotter (e.g., Shotter, 1997b) and Arlene Katz (Katz & Shotter, 1996, 1997) here, and I gratefully acknowledge their work. They write of a form of social poetics based on Wittgensteinian methods that offers us some useful authorial tools. It is particularly pertinent here that Wittgenstein himself saw his methods as belonging in the aesthetic realm: "Philosophy ought really to be written only as a poetic composition" (1980, p. 24). John Shotter described four practical poetic methods that are drawn from our everyday use of talk (1997b). It is perhaps important to emphasize here, in advance, that these methods are not for systematic application to arrive at a coherent connected picture. They are tools we can use as the moments call for them, in any way we choose.

The first method is to ask "What are we struck by?" Wittgenstein (1953, nos. 132, 144) tell us to "stop", "look", and "listen to this." Rather than trying to think about what may be going on, we need to attend to what actually is going on and what we are most struck by. In some ways, we could say a good primary researcher is most easily struck by things. This requires that sense of awe and wonder I talked about in chapter 7 and earlier in this chapter in relation to dialogic listening and appreciative inquiry. I provide an extended illustration of the use of this struck by tool in the next chapter. But it might help here to briefly show how I used it in the appreciative inquiry into organizational communication practices I described earlier in this chapter.

To start off the first inquiry session I told the participants that I had been struck by three things. My talking of went along these lines (based on preparatory notes—not actual words):

Struck by how well they managed change
I've a great deal of respect for how they have managed so well in the face of enormous change in the organization. I can well appreciate that there is some residual confusion and uncertainty because of this. Sometimes this confusion and uncertainty is downright healthy, keeping you open to new ways of doing things.

Struck by healthy cynicism needing balance
I've also observed much healthy cynicism in the organization, but I want to help balance this with a sense of hope for better things in the future. Luckily, I've also been struck by enough expressions of hope for positive outcomes that I'm sure we can achieve this balance.

Struck by awareness of communication
I've also been struck by the degree of awareness about the importance of improving communication practices, and everyone's willingness to talk about it.

The second poetic method requires us to attend to the metaphors. What metaphors are being used? How are dead metaphors (see Lakoff & Johnson, 1980) obscuring other possible understandings? How can new metaphors offer new possibilities or reveal what has been hidden? When we ask these questions, however, we are not trying to plumb the real or true meaning of what someone is trying to say. We are instead, as Rorty (1989) pointed out, simply trying to place it in a particular language game.

Our metaphors about language and communication provide a particularly pertinent and powerful example. When talking about limited views of communication in various chapters, I have mentioned the idea of a conduit metaphor. In that metaphor, words are taken to be packages for our ideas that we take out of our heads and then transmit to others who, in turn, take the ideas out of the word packages and put them into their heads (Reddy, 1979). This metaphor takes communication to be nothing more than a mechanical transmission process. In contrast, consider the possibilities of thinking about communication using ecological or environmental metaphors.

I was first drawn to the possibility of this metaphor and the alternative language game it generated when I was asked to help with research into the communication practices of a commission responsible for the management of our largest inland water system, covering five (out of eight) of our Australian states and territories. Ecological and environmental concepts abounded in their concerns, and it struck me as I was listening to them talk about the communication issues they faced that they might find it useful to think about these issues environmentally. I developed the notion of a communication environment in the following way, and the members of the commission found it particularly powerful in helping them see the complexity of the process and the many interrelationships they had to take into consideration.

The environment metaphor emphasizes that:
- *We live in communication, just as we live in a physical enviroment.*
- *Our communicative environment is as complex as our physical environment.*

- *The ecology of this communicative environment is created out of the communicative practices in which we engage.*
- *We can manage our communicative environment in a sustainable manner or otherwise.*
- *But, unlike the physical environment, we (as human beings) cannot have control over our communicative environment (that consists of other human beings).*

The participants and activities in this environment involve:
- *Multiple partners, with different needs and responsibilities.*
- *Multiple positions, with different views.*
- *Discontinuous relationships and occluded views.*
- *The major thing we do in this environment is jointly create meanings/understandings.*
- *Meanings emerge out of the various relationships with multiple partners in multiple positions—thus, they are variable and manifold.*
- *The context in which meaning is generated is critical—we make sense in our environment.*

The third Wittgensteinian method calls for us to make comparisons. We need to ask: "What comparisons can be made to show order and contrasts?" By order, I do not mean, nor did Wittgenstein, the hidden, real order; rather, it is an order that may be useful for an understanding that allows us to proceed. One helpful way of making comparisons is to attend to how the participants in the research process are the same and different. Another way, suggested by Wittgenstein, is to invent an object of comparison (1953, no. 130) to explore possible orders. Using Wittgenstein's idea of a language game, you could ask: "What if I change the language game and talk about it like this?" In one sense, this is what I did with the communication-as-environment metaphor illustrated earlier.

Another particularly compelling example of changing the language to make comparisons was illustrated in some work of Sallyann Roth and David Epston (1996a, 1996b). In our everyday talk we typically employ what they called "problem-internalizing questions." We use questions that address the person and the problem as the one thing (e.g., "How long have you been depressed?" or "Have you been afraid all your life?"). It should be pointed out that this doesn't just apply to people with psychological problems. We also use it on other contexts (e.g., "How long has your organization had difficulties with customer relations?" or "How long has your company had that communication problem?").

In comparison, Roth and Epston suggested trying problem-externalizing questions. In doing this, their aim was "to create linguistic and relational contexts in which people experiencing themselves as burdened, crushed, or taken over by problems can imagine and activate alternative and preferred relationships with these problems" (Roth & Epston, 1996a, p. 151). Problem-externalizing examples they offered include: "What has Demoralisation talked you into about yourself?" and "As you tell it, Fears have really been pushing you around for the last year or so" (1996a, p. 149). Outside of the therapeutic value of these questions, they illustrate a particularly powerful, alternative language game.

The fourth Wittgensteinian method calls for making connections. We need to ask questions like: "What connections can be made?", "How are things connected to other things?" Or, more to the point, "How does our talk show interconnectedness?" We arrive at these connections using any or all of the other methods described previously. In this Wittgensteinian view, making connections is a different type of understanding. It is not an understanding that seeks causes and explanations, nor is it an understanding that simply describes; instead it is an active understanding that sees connections, and thus allows us to anticipate possibilities for how to go on. Making connections is essentially an aesthetic consideration.

In one sense, the whole thrust of this book has been about making such connections; especially those new connections that arise when you change the language game. I have been concerned with changing the language game about communicating and with asking: "What happens if I talk about it like this?" As I pointed out at the end of chapter 3, in making the grammatical shift from nouns (*communication*) to verbs and gerunds (*communicating*) I shifted into a new language game. That change was the first step in evolving a new grammar, or way of talking, about communicating that was progressively developed over the ensuing chapters.

Reembodying the telling

Whether we are doing our telling of to other participants or to others outside the primary process, the best and most important data we have is the lived experience. I discussed the importance of returning to the lived experience in chapter 4, in reference to the work of John Dewey. But it is equally important in the work of Wittgenstein just described. In both Wittgenstein's and Dewey's views, the focus of our attention needs to be on our practices, on our lived moments of interaction. In contrast, the more we move away from the lived experience to abstract notions, composite pictures, or aggregated data the more we are moving away from the real—from our experiencing.

This argument is particularly important when we come to telling of our primary research experiences to others. The more we use examples, quotes, and stories in our texts the more alive and the more understandable it becomes to others. This is because in our attempts to capture the orality of the experience we are attempting to capture our humanity, not develop abstract theory. Using examples and stories in other people's words maintains our good faith with the participatory process and with the four moves of Toulmin's I discussed in chapter 2 and reintroduced in chapter 7. Reembodying the telling honors the moves to the local, to the timely, to the oral, and to the particular.

When I first started to develop the idea of primary, participatory research and talked about the need to capture experience, a friend pondered:

> What would our discipline be like if our journals were filled with partic-
> ipatory research such as described by Penman? How would articles be
> written that focus on possibilities, that stress their effect in enabling
> both researcher and those studied to keep their experiences open and
> to deal empirically with their lived experience, and that acknowledge
> their own role in constructing the world in which we live? (Pearce,
> 1994a, p. 11)

I confess that, at the time, I wondered myself. And I am still wondering. There can never be one or any complete answer to those questions. Indeed, we have barely just begun to explore what could be done. So the field is wide open to creative possibilities.

9

Practical inquiry in our daily lives

The last sentence in the last chapter was a tempting place to finish—such a wonderfully open ending, inviting all manner of possibilities. But to stop there would not, in the end, be acting in good faith with you, the reader. You may recall that in chapter 5 I talked about this issue of open-endedness and the need for some form of closure, however temporary. Good closure provides us with an aesthetic experience, that momentary understanding of the pattern and structure of experience that allows us to go on. I want to attempt such a good closure here by pulling together a number of the previous arguments in such a way that you can see how you might go on, using the tools of practical inquiry in your daily life.

Over the last 3 centuries a great divide has been constructed between how we understand our daily experience of living and how scientists understand (or discover) the facts of life. Our ordinary, everyday understandings in the particular contexts of our experience have been denied in favor of those of the scientific expert. Unfortunately, the scientific expert is constrained to utterances of an abstract and global form that have little bearing on what we do daily and how we can lead the good life.

This whole book is premised on the denial of such conventional, scientific knowledge and the assertion of the material, or foundational, nature of communicating—the third choice I talked about in chapter 2. With this third choice, we are able to directly face the practical problems of our world and ask, from the position of participation, what we can do. Well, let's look at some of the things we might do. In what follows, I illustrate some of the research practices and tools described in earlier chapters with two very different case studies. Not all aspects of the studies will be presented, only extracts to illustrate points and show possibilities.

✍ An inquiry into the possibility of dialogue

Here, I want to draw on elements of an unpublished study that illustrate a way of inquiring into the possibility of and, at the same time, the setting up of a community dialogue process. In 1997, I was approached by an international banking group to help them establish "a more formal process of dialogue and engagement" with community groups. Their desire for dialogue was exciting to me (even if I experienced some disbelief). On the other hand, their wish to improve relations with communities had to be seen in the context of recent surveys indicating that the majority of banking customers do not trust banks.

Understanding full well the complexities, sensitivities, and potential problems, I knew that I had to do very careful preparatory work. I talked about a set of preparatory tools in the last chapter. Here I illustrate how they were employed for this project with the bank. In this particular instance, the preparatory work was the critical part of the whole practical inquiry process. This is part of what I told the bank I would do:

> In order to develop a more formal process of dialogue and engagement with the community, we will need to explore what you have already set in place for the community program, what contacts with representative groups have been made, and what the nature of the discussions have been. We are particularly concerned to understand exactly what the bank is trying to achieve with these processes and what, in turn, the community could want from the bank. As part of this, we will want to talk with some of the representative groups you have already contacted. In talking with them, we will investigate processes that may best suit those groups.
>
> The outcome will be a sketch of the current communication environment of your organization. This sketch will identify the

constraints on communication practices and indicate the possible pathways for developing better processes. This report will also contain a detailed project proposal for achieving the aims of developing a more formal process of dialogue and engagement. The proposal will be based on the most useful contemporary thinking in communication. We estimate that we will need to spend 2 days with various members of your staff in the head office, gathering some of the data we will need and setting up meetings with other staff and community members. In addition, we will need to spend 2 days talking with community groups. Following this preliminary investigative round we are likely to need to spend another day with you and your staff to clarify issues.

In essence, what I laid out for them here was the backbone for a primary research process. The first stage in this process was to talk with potential participants in the proposed dialogue. To do this talking, I prepared a set of questions, drawing on the tools of rehearsal and anticipation described in the last chapter. Here are the questions for the different types of people I had to talk with—please note the appreciative orientation.

I spoke individually with three bank managers in the corporate relations area and six representatives from community groups, using the following questions as my guide (but not necessarily adhering to the order or the wording):

Questions for the bank managers

- *Tell me your vision for the community project.*
- *What would be a good outcome for the first stage of this project? For the organization? For the communities?*
- *What is your sense of dialogue and engagement?*
- *What organizational issues/sensitivities need we be alert for?*
- *Who are the likely community participants? Who has already been approached? Who else should be? Are there any communities to be excluded/less important than others? What do you already know about these communities? What may be good ways of proceeding?*
- *What are the practical constraints—e.g., budget allocation for community consultation, and organizational resources available for it?*
- *In what ways can they best help us achieve good outcomes for this project?*

Questions for the community groups

- *What involvement have you had to date? With the banking industry? With the bank?*
- *What do you understand the bank's intentions to be about this community project?*
- *Tell me your vision for the community project. What would be the good things for the community that could come of it? What could be the good things for the banking industry or the bank?*
- *How would you like the project to proceed? What could be good ways for bringing about this vision? How would you know that they are good ways?*
- *Who are other good community participants to get involved in this project?*

Conversational themes

Historical context.   One of the significant understandings that came out of these conversations was the importance of the historical context. The community group representatives painted an unfortunate picture of their history of conversations with banks. As one person put it: "The banking industry is still in the conflict mode of the 80s—they have never really overcome an adversarial relationship with consumers." Others felt as though they had made positive approaches over a number of years to no avail: "We've put out the olive branch over a number of years." Yet others believed that they are simply not listened to: "Our reasoning is simply rejected."

From all of the community groups, I got the sense that their history with the banking industry makes them wary. On the other hand, because issues related to banking are centrally important, they know they must continue to be involved in any conversations of importance to their group. Both the wariness arising from history and the preparedness to continue engagement had to be recognized in developing new processes. In particular, as one person put it, although "recent consultations with the bank have been impressive, the doubt will continue for quite awhile yet."

There is a further factor, however, that had to be taken into account when considering the historical context of conversations between communities and banks. As one of the community representatives suggested, the reasoning frameworks have been incompatible. From the point of view of the banks, community groups have been "economically unrealistic." From the point of view of the community, banks have been "economically greedy." Constructive conversations cannot take place within such incommensurate frameworks. So it was critical that another sense-making frame was chosen/offered for any future conversations to proceed well.

What did community groups want? From our conversations with the community groups, it was clear that they are dissatisfied with a range of conversational approaches. Below are some of their descriptions of the conversational modes they found to be particularly unproductive:

> Friendly chats where people agree to disagree; along with a show of corporate muscle.
>
> Agenda fully set and constrained by the corporation.
>
> Incommensurable frameworks clashing.
>
> The outcome of the conversation is a foregone conclusion.
>
> The model used in consumer advice forums or customer councils where advice is given and ignored.

It was clear that the old paradigm based on a confrontational model had not been successful, nor was the paradigm based on a facade of consulting. In exploring other possible ways of communicating, the community groups made a number of concrete suggestions. Interestingly, all these suggestions pointed to a desire for the sort of dialogue described in chapter 6. These suggestions, using their words, included:

> Important to ensure that all participants understand what the meetings will be about and how they will be run and that all participants agree to the process in advance.
>
> Need to develop the conversation slowly, spend time developing a framework for understanding, looking at the big picture first.
>
> The orientation is towards opening up the conversation, not damage control.
>
> Must be a genuine two-way process.
>
> Any proposal and agreement to proceed must be mutual and binding on all sides.

There was a range of opinions about what the conversational process could be about, and who should be involved. It was this area that showed the most discrepancies between the different groups. The possibilities raised included such items as (again using their words):

Issues related directly to banking with the aim of informing the groups as early as possible about any changes.

Broader issues confronting the various community groups and thus requiring involvement of generalist groups, such as those you talked with for this stage of the project and the bank staff.

Specific issues from a specific community [not the representative body] that senior bank executives should know about and understand.

Specific technical issues that need resolving between specialists and senior bank staff.

The discussions with groups also pointed to the importance of clearly establishing what the criteria for a good outcome would be. With this criteria established, the group itself could then determine the success or otherwise of the process. The type of criteria suggested by the groups included:

A change in approach to looking after the smaller customer.

A clear recognition that the reasoning frameworks of the group is well grounded in reality.

The bank supports, or pursues, at least one community initiative every 12–18 months. [This will be] a show of good faith.

Sticking points. Establishing a genuine dialogic process is never easy, and can never be controlled by any one person—it requires the goodwill of all involved. So an essential first step is generating that good will. However, I anticipated a number of sticking points in this process of generating goodwill and in attempting to follow the dialogue paradigm.

First, although the external relations managers believed that the senior executive banking staff needed to be involved in this process, these were likely to be people with little understanding (or desire) of how to engage in a new paradigm of communicating based on dialogue. In addition, some of the community groups expressed concern about interacting with senior executive banking staff. Although they had learned to feel comfortable with the bank staff they had met, they retained their strong wariness of what they called "real banking staff." This suggested the need for important premeeting work with the senior banking staff before they joined the community dialogue.

Second, some of the community groups were also likely to be unprepared or unwilling to engage in dialogue. Their representatives were professional in their job of representation and this often meant they would insist on speaking for their group alone. This again suggested the need for specific premeeting preparation, especially about the rules of engagement and the need to speak from their own experiences, not as a representative of a constituency.

Third, although the different community groups shared the same general needs for a demonstration of good faith, their expectations about the topic and purpose of any conversation varied. Whereas the bank wanted a broad dialogue about community issues, this was not endorsed by all groups. Some of the groups wanted to focus on specific banking issues only, such as to be informed in a timely manner or to engage in discussion about the issues. This suggested that there may be a need for a series of complementing conversational activities with different degrees of generality and different levels of banking staff. This possibility could either be explored as part of the initial dialogue meetings (i.e., what other conversational forms may be desirable, with whom) or as part of the premeeting work.

Fourth, the community groups who expressed a willingness to be involved and those others proposed by the bank, were all peak lobby groups, well removed from their actual communities. Although their views were impor-tant, they could not necessarily give the full flavor of what it is to be, say, part of the Chinese ethnic community, or an elderly person. This suggested the need to consider other means by which grass-roots members of the commun-ities could make a contribution to the conversation.

What happened?

Much of the textual material around the themes just discussed came directly from reports I wrote to the bank. All of these written reports were part of our preparatory work. We were undergoing a continuing negotiation and, to some extent, management of meaning process. At the end of the report partly quoted earlier, we required an agreement from the bank to proceed with setting up the process—once again negotiating their commitment.

In the end, we agreed to establish two different groups to cater to the different community needs. One group was designed for the possibility of dialogue, the other to concentrate on more concrete, issue-oriented talk. Rules of engagement were designed to reflect these different aims, and a further round of negotiations followed to agree on the rules. In all, there were three rounds of negotiations/preparatory work before the groups started.

⟪ An inquiry into information needs in a medical context

In this second illustration, we were concerned with providing information that could help people get the most out of taking medicine. I've chosen this example to illustrate how, out of primary research, we can generate new and better ways of doing things.

The issue of concern here was how to support HIV/AIDS patients on a triple-combination drug therapy regimen. This triple-combination regimen is an extremely complex one, and at the time of the project (1997–8) it was still in its experimental stage. We needed to develop an information support program that took these critical factors into account and provided information that made sense in the daily lives of patients on this regimen—that is, in their lived experience. The work described here was led by one of my colleagues at the Communication Research Institute, Maureen Mackenzie-Taylor, and was documented in Mackenzie-Taylor (1997a, 1997b, 1997c).

As a starting point in this investigation, we needed to understand about the information needs and the contexts of use—for both the information and the drugs—of these patients. Specifically, we needed to know things like:

- *What is the language they use to talk about the medicines and their problems?*
- *What does taking these medicines mean to them?*
- *How does taking a triple-combination therapy fit into the daily context of their lifestyle?*
- *What makes the triple-combination therapy difficult to comply with?*
- *To what extent does existing information meet users' needs?*
- *How can we provide information in more appropriate ways so that people can make informed decisions about how to act and whether to comply?*

In our first round of inquiries, we were concerned to keep our conversations as open as possible to allow for personal engagement with our participants, and to facilitate collaboration in generating better ways of providing information support for them. This was very important to us, and to our inquiry, knowing that we were working with people who were ill and likely to be under a great deal of physical and emotional stress. In listening to our participants, we also were conscious that the tools of Wittgenstein, described in the last chapter, could prove very useful; particularly, what we were struck by and the patients' language use.

Conversational themes

Talking about drugs and the therapeutic regimen.　Our first two question topics were oriented to understanding the patient's point of view about the triple-combination therapy. It became clear in our conversations that our participants were keenly aware that they were involved in the development of new treatments for HIV—many spoke of being "human guinea pigs." They were also aware that the scientific/medical understandings of these treatments change rapidly. However, they did not know which information to trust, or how new research would effect them personally. Yet, they needed this information in order to be able to make decisions and choices so that they could control their lives.

Control was a constant theme in our conversations. Having the right information, as well as being able to stop treatment, gave a sense of control, as these participants' statements show:

> One of the scary things about being ill is feeling that you've lost control. Its not being told what to do, but being given options and having control and independence.

> To know what foods are good and not good with your drugs is incredibly empowering.

> Diet is one of the things we can control.

> During the period of trying to get into the routine I stressed myself out too much . . . . I decided I had to control my life and I stopped it [the treatment].

Another theme that struck us as very important was reflected in the recurrent use of the word *commitment*.

> Long term survival taught me the art of discipline. If you commit and take control, you can get back into life.

When we heard the way the word *commitment* was being used, it opened up a new understanding for us. In medical contexts, we are always hearing drug companies and doctors talk about problems with patient compliance. Indeed this was how we were presented with the problem—as one of improving compliance. On reflection, the word *compliance* was obviously from a traditional medical context—patients have to comply with doctors' orders. Given the need of these HIV/AIDS patients to take control, offering them the chance to commit was far more appropriate. We took this notion of commitment and control as two major themes in the development of supportive information materials.

Understanding the therapy in the context of patient lifestyle. We were struck by a number of things in these conversations that powerfully illuminated the difficulties in these people's lives and their need for inform-ation that made sense for them. One of the most difficult issues for them related to the relationship between taking the drugs and eating. One of the drugs (indinivar) had a critical dose window of 3 hours, in which only very light, low-fat, or no food could be eaten, and it had to be taken 3 times a day. The difficulties this created are reflected in these participants' comments:

> Straddling indinivar around food puts me off starting.

> If you forget to take your pill before you eat breakfast you have to wait 2 hours before you can take it. That puts you out of step by 2 hours all day—its very late at night before you can take the last dose—it leads to sleep deprivation.

> Hunger forces mess-ups.

> The eating pattern impacts on my day. I have to negotiate it constantly.

> Dieticians recommend that AIDS patients eat often and frequently to avoid overloading. We develop habits of eating light grazing meals. But having to take indinivar on an empty stomach every 8 hours, and not eat high protein/fat food for 2 hours after, it means there are 9 hours out of our 16 waking hours that we cannot eat for, so we can't eat enough to maintain our weight.

These people had to take at least seven different tablets/doses a day and going out or traveling created special difficulties for them, as this patient said:

> If I'm away for a couple of days I put all the pills in one bottle, but its a real challenge sorting out what to take when.

Yet, despite the difficulties, we were struck by so many positive, practical approaches to managing them. Here are some of them:

> I keep my midday dose in an antique pill box my partner gave me. It gives me pleasure each time I use it.

> I make it a ritual. I use little sake cups to sort my pills out each day—a

different cup for each dose. Why open and close so many little bottles three times a day?

If you understand the value of treatment and are fully committed to it [pill taking], it allows you to see yourself as an advocate rather than a victim and taking pills in public can become like a badge of honor—a bit like coming out.

Because of these people's needs for information and to take control of their lives, we collected anecdotes and tips, including those quoted earlier, to form part of our information support program. Not only did these anecdotes and tips act to help understanding in the daily context of their lived experiences, but they articulated the voice of the people on triple-combination therapy to help others also on it. This sidestepped the complaint of "I'm sick of being told what to do" and offered help from within the community.

Misunderstandings and information needs.   Even though we were collaborating with a sophisticated and information-hungry group, there were many misunderstandings about the best way to follow the treatment regimen. There are three critical components of the regimen; the relation between eating/not eating and taking the drugs, taking the drugs every 8 hours, and drinking a lot of fluid. Most people understood these components in terms of the medical reasoning, but not how it could be applied in their everyday lives. The information they had been getting lacked specificity and applicability.

Following are some of the questions people asked that signaled they could not use the medical information to make practical decisions:

What do I do if I only remember a dose 3 hours after I should have taken it? Do I skip it or take it? If I take it, should I adjust the time of my next dose?

What do I do if taking a particular dose would interfere with special social plans? Do I take it when convenient or skip it altogether?

What can I order in a restaurant if I arrive there close to my dose time?

The medical information on these issues only focused on best practice— that is, the right dose, at the right time, in the right way. It did not allow for the variable and often complex demands of patients' daily lives, nor did it recognize the way patients' wanted to understand the information in terms of how it help to them to act (or otherwise). Our response to this problem was to develop descriptions of different levels of acceptability—ideal, good, and bad practice. The word *ideal* suggests something to aspire to but not always attainable; whereas *good* confirms that although the practices are not the best they are still acceptable. When we tested this approach, people welcomed the recognition of their difficulties in trying to meet the ideal, and felt empowered to take control and make acceptable choices of how to act.

Reflections on this inquiry

When we conduct practical inquiries of this sort, we do so from the position of participation with our partners. We work with them to generate information that helps them act well in their everyday lives. We are, in essence, coconstructing meaning that makes sense for them (especially sense that allows action). We know we have done it well, in terms of sense-making, because we keep on working with our partners until they actually say it make sense for them. In this way, the ultimate judgment of good practice resides in the users of the information using it in their practice. But we are only able to do this because we also adopt the practice of good process.

I chose this illustration in part because it was such a good process. All of the collaborators enjoyed doing this work. When you can spend all day talking intensively (working dialogically) often with very ill people and finish the day feeling almost exhilarated, you know it has gone well. Although this is far from any conventional scientific criteria, it is one that I have progressively relied on to indicate the quality of the meanings generated (discussed earlier in chapter 7). It is exactly the same criteria we use when we say we've had a good conversation. How do we know? Because we felt engaged and alive with the other!

I also chose this illustration because it reflects the value and power of reembodying the telling. In the various information materials we developed to support patients on the triple-combination treatment regimen, we drew extensively on their anecdotes, hints, and tips. We retold the story using their voices. But this was not for the purposes of mere description; instead it was to bring about new possibilities for others.

⟨Ɑ Constructing futures

Although the two illustrations of research had very different concerns, they share a method: a mode of inquiry in the primary research position I discussed in chapter 7. Rather than drawing solely on past knowledge, theory, or research facts and providing solutions directly, we entered the domain of inquiry and asked the people concerned how to best to proceed for them. These conversations generated a practical knowing, a concept first introduced in chapter 4. You may recall that there I drew on Aristotle's distinctions among scientific, productive, and practical knowledge, where the latter was concerned with doing things. In both of the illustrations, we were concerned with generating knowledge (or understandings) for doing things—for dialoguing and for informing in context. Although all the material in this book directs us on how we may proceed for doing things, there are several key factors that deserve highlighting and further the point of temporary closure.

Avoiding the search for the solution

In the first chapter of this book I mentioned John Saul's (1992) passionate plea to discard the frantic search for answers and to start asking questions. The frantic search for answers he referred to is the search for scientific and technical knowledge to provide solutions to human problems. Perhaps the most profoundly disturbing example of this frantic search is a knowledge database project I recently heard about (and am still hoping is only an urban myth). The aim of this project, commissioned by the United Nations, is a computer data-base that will record all the world's problems and solutions! Can you imagine that once this is completed we will have the solution for everything? Not likely, given the infinitely creative and often wonderfully perverse nature of human beings.

In following through the constructionist arguments here, it becomes obvious, at least to me, that each so-called problem we are confronted with is unique. This notion has been delightfully captured in the wicked problem approach to design, first formulated by Horst Rittel in the 1960s. He coined the idea of wicked problems as an alternative to the linear thinking being used by most designers of that time (and today). Essentially, linear thinking entailed two major phases: problem definition and problem solution. In the problem definition phase, all the elements of the problem are systematically analysed; whereas in the solution phase, these elements are synthesized into a solution. Many people still use this linear thinking approach today, believing that it offers the only hope of a logical solution to a problem—whether it be of design or otherwise.

Rittell argued that most of the problems faced by designers could not be addressed by this linear approach, because most of these were "wicked problems." Wicked problems are a "class of social systems problems which are ill-formulated, where the information is confusing, where there are many clients and decision-makers with conflicting values, and where the ramifications in the whole system are thoroughly confusing" (cited in Buchanan, 1995, p. 14).

Some of the features of wicked problems are:

- They can be described in different ways and have different solutions—there is no one way to formulate the problem.
- The solutions to wicked problems cannot be true or false, although they can be good or bad.
- There is always more than one plausible explanation for a wicked problem.
- There is no single right or true test for a solution to a wicked problem.
- Every wicked problem is unique.

One of the wickedly exciting things about the idea of a wicked problem is that it describes all manner of communicative activities, whether they be an ordinary conversation, planning and running a community discussion, enhancing organizational communication processes, or designing a document. The very processural and dynamic features of communicating means that nothing is ever certain in the process; meanings and understandings change and develop as communicating proceeds and as the participants and their contexts change. Communicating is an inherently messy and uncertain process that can never be controlled, resolved, or contained.

Recognizing communicating as a wicked problem has a number of ramifications. First, it is not possible to define exactly what the problem is in communicating. Although those in a particular communicative context may feel uneasy about the nature of the communication practices, to try and find the definitive source, or nature of the problem is not possible. We are always constructing our meaning or problem definition out of the process we are engaged in—that is, out of communicating. So there can be as many different problem definitions as participants in the process. Moreover, as the process continues and new meanings emerge, so too can new problem definitions. These multiple and changing meanings reflect the inherently uncertain nature of communicating mentioned previously.

Second, it is not possible to come up with the one right solution to a wicked communicating problem. As I said in the last chapter when discussing appreciative inquiry, there are as many different possible right solutions as there are participants who think they have defined the right problem. The trick is not to try to find the right solution, but instead to look for a possible pathway that seems good for the participants, the organization, or the community. We need not ask what is the solution to the problem, but instead what we can do to go on.

Third, the only way to test whether the solution to a wicked communicating problem is a good one is to practice it. It is not possible to stand back from the proposal and apply an objective, independent test of it. Instead, you must engage in the process and assess it as it proceeds. Does it allow you and others to do things you class as good? Does it open up new possibilities for you?

Fourth, every wicked communicating problem is unique. What worked in one context, with certain participants, will not necessarily work with other participants in other contexts. Trying to bring about good practices means you always have to be monitoring what is happening and be prepared to be flexible in what you do. This is the core of practical inquiry in communicating— monitoring and changing, not controlling.

When I talk about communicating as a wicked problem in this way, many people become concerned that they should not be avoiding problem-solution talk altogether. They plead that surely we have to work out what the problems are before we can find a solution. Indeed, in the organizational communicating inquiry I used to illustrate points in chapter 8, this problem talk became a sticking point. As one participant expressed it, "If I don't know what the problems are, how can I come up with a solution?"

You may recall that in the last chapter I mentioned the need to avoid problem talk when I was discussing the approach of appreciative inquiry (an approach developed specifically to challenge the traditional problem-solving approach in organizational change processes). In contrast, appreciative inquiry is oriented to finding what an organization does well and helping it do more of what works (Hammond, 1996). There is no doubt that this orientation to appreciate the positive provides new openings and possibilities in conversations. Nevertheless, to argue that we avoid problem-solution talk in all circumstances would be to treat the wicked problem of communicating as a simple linear one; that is, as always having the same solution (of avoiding problems). On the other hand, to become obsessed with finding the problem and the solution is to equally treat the wicked problem of communicating as a simple linear one.

Sometimes we may need to talk about problems and solutions, but it is important to keep in mind that there are as many ways of defining a problem and as many solutions. We need not try to find the right one; instead, we should focus on what good options we have to proceed with communicating. Good options would keep the participants involved and enable them to do things with their communicating. Good options would open up new possibilities for participants—good options construct futures, not answers.

Asking questions, in good faith

In the end, our way forward relies on the questions we ask. It is our questions that generate new possibilities, or at least they should be doing so—with all the moral import that *should* implies. In chapter 7, I discussed the relationship between questions and accomplishments. The word *accomplishment* was very carefully chosen to both sidestep the concept of "solution" and to point to how questions bring things about.

The form of questioning needed in primary research practice preserves an orientation to openness and prevents premature closure. This form of questioning is also that required for dialogic listening; it involves genuine curiosity and is designed to open up the other's talking. This form of questioning is also oriented to experience and practice in our everyday lives. Can you imagine what new futures may be in store for us if we asked more of this form of question? Most important, this form of questioning is questioning done in good faith.

The notions of good faith and moral knowing have been twin themes throughout this book. For me, these intertwined concepts provide the necessary radical departure from the rationalist's quest for truth and scientific knowledge. By *radical* here, I mean "getting to the root of", for the roots of understanding communicating are in the process of doing it. This is essentially the same argument that ran through chapter 5, when I considered the means for evaluating the process of communicating: The means for understanding reside in the very process itself. There is just no getting out of it.

What we know and do comes out of our experience in the process of communicating. It was that recognition many years ago that drove me onward to explore what all that could mean. Curiously, it has seemed to lead to a simpler, yet less sure, way of understanding. Even as I was writing this book, with the progression of chapters, I could slough off the more abstract, the more technical, and the more seemingly academic mode and return to a simpler way of talking. However, this simpler way is not an easy way. Indeed, it is a way that leads into unchartered waters. Yet, at the same time, it is a way that, to return to chapter 1, helps explore new constellations, create new horizons, and ask new questions.

What counts fundamentally in all these explorations is acting in good faith, with both the process and the participants in it. We may no longer have all the measurement tools of scientists, or the metaphorical labcoat to hide behind, but we have something far more important—our good faith with humanity, and our capacity to act truly.

☾☉ References

Anderson, R., Cissna, K., & Arnett, R. (Eds.). (1994). *The reach of dialogue: Confirmation, voice, and community.* Cresskill, NJ: Hampton.

Avery, R. K., & Eadie, W. F. (1993). Making a difference in the real world. *Journal of Communication, 43*(3), 174–179.

Bakhtin, M. M. (1990). *Art and answerability: Early philosophical essays by M. M. Bakhtin* (M. Holquist & V. Liapunov, Eds.). Austin: University of Texas Press.

Bauman, Z. (1991). The social manipulation of morality: Moralizing actors, adiaphorizing action. *Theory, Culture & Society, 8,* 137–151.

Becker, C., Chasin, L., Herzig, M., & Roth, S. (1995). From stuck debate to new conversation on controversial issues. *Journal of Feminist Family Therapy, 7*(1-2), 143–163.

Beniger, J. R. (1993). Communication—embrace the subject not the field. *Journal of Communication, 43*(3), 18–25.

Bennett, T. (1987). Really useless "knowledge": A political critique of aesthetics. *Literature and History, 13,* 8–57.

Bennett, W. (1985). Communication and social responsiblity. *Quarterly Journal of Speech, 71,* 259–288.

Berger, P. L., & Luckman, T. (1967). *The social construction of reality.* Garden City, NY: Doubleday/Anchor.

Bernstein, R. J. (1983). *Beyond objectivism and relativism.* Oxford, England: Basil Blackwell.

Bernstein, R. J. (1992). *The new constellation.* Cambridge, MA: MIT Press.

Billig, M. (1987). *Arguing and thinking: A rhetorical approach to social psychology.* Cambridge, England: Cambridge University Press.

Bohm, D. (1996). *On dialogue* (L. Nichol, Ed.). London: Routledge.

Bruner, J. (1975). The ontogenesis of speech acts. *Journal of Child Language, 2,* 1–21.

Buber, M. (1958). *I and thou* (2nd ed.; R. G. Smith, Trans.). New York: Charles Scribner's Sons.

Buber, M. (1965). *Between man and man* (R. G. Smith, Trans.). New York: Macmillan.

Buchanan, R. (1995). Myth and maturity: Toward a new order in the decade of design. In V. Margolin & R. Buchanan (Eds.), *The idea of design* (pp. 75–85). Cambridge, MA: MIT Press.

Burleson, B., & Kline, S. (1979). Habermas' theory of communication: A critical explication. *Quarterly Journal of Speech, 65,* 412–428.

Campbell, R. (1992). *Truth & historicity.* Oxford, England: Clarendon Press.

Cappella, J. (1990). The method of proof by example in interaction analysis. *Communication Monographs, 57,* 236–240.

Cissna, K., & Anderson, R. (1994). Communication and the ground of dialogue. In R. Anderson, K. Cissna, & R. Arnett (Eds.), *The reach of dialogue: Confirmation, voice, and community* (pp. 9–30). Cresskill, NJ: Hampton.

Cissna, K., & Anderson, R. (1998). Theorizing about dialogic moments: The Buber–Rogers position and postmodern themes. *Communication Theory, 8,* 63–104.

Cooperrider, D., & Srivasta, S. (1987). Appreciative inquiry in organisational life. *Research in Organisational Change and Development, 1,* 129–169.

Copleston, F. (1985). *A history of philosophy: Book two.* New York: Image Books.

Craig, R. T. (1993). Why are there so many communication theories? *Journal of Communication, 43*(3), 26–33.

Craig, R. T. (1995). Foreword. In W. Leeds-Hurwitz (Ed.), *Social approaches to communication* (pp. v–ix). New York: Guilford.

Craig, R. T. (1999). Communication theory as a field. *Communication Theory, 9,* 119–161.

Craig, R. T. & Tracy, K. (1995). Grounded practical theory: The case for intellectual discussion. *Communication Theory, 5*(3), 248–272.

Cronen, V. (1995a). Practical theory and the tasks ahead for social approaches to communication. In W. Leeds-Hurwitz (Ed.), *Social Approaches to Communication* (pp. 217–242). New York: Guilford.

Cronen, V. (1995b). Coordinated management of meaning: The consequentiality of communication and the recapturing of experience. In S. Sigman (Ed.), *The consequentiality of communication* (pp. 17–66). Hillsdale, NJ: Lawrence Erlbaum & Associates.

Cronen, V., & Lang, P. (1994). Language and action: Wittgenstein and Dewey in the practice of therapy and consultation. *Human Systems, 5,* 5–43.

Dance, F. E. X. (1970). The "concept" of communication. *Journal of Communication, 20,* 210–210.

Davies, T. (1987). The ark in flames: Science, language and education in seventeenth-century England. In A. Benjamin, G. Cantor & J. Christie (Eds.), *The figural and the literal: Problems of language in the history of science and philosophy* (pp. 1630–1800). Manchester, England: Manchester University Press.

Davis, F. K., & Jasinski, J. (1993). Beyond the cultural wars: An agenda for research on communciation and culture. *Journal of Communication, 43*(3), 141–149.

Deetz, S. A. (1994). Future of the discipline: The challenges, the research, and the social contribution. In S. A. Deetz (Ed.), *Communication yearbook 17* (pp. 565–600). Thousand Oaks, CA: Sage.

Derrida, J. (1977). *Of grammatology* (G. C. Spivak, Trans.). Baltimore, MD: Johns Hopkins University Press.

Dervin, B. (1993). Verbing communicating: Mandate for disciplinary intervention. *Journal of Communication, 43*(3), 45–54.

Dewey, J. (1934). *Art and experience.* New York: Capricorn.

Dewey, J. (1981). *The philosophy of John Dewey* (J. McDermott, Ed.). Chicago: University of Chicago Press.

Docherty, D., Morrison, D., & Tracey, M. (1993). Scholarship as silence. *Journal of Communication, 43*(3), 230–238.

Ellinor, L., & Gerard, G. (1998). *Dialogue: Rediscover the transforming power of conversation.* New York: Wiley.

Feyerabend, P. (1975). *Against method.* London: NLB.

Fiske, J. (1982). *Introduction to communication studies.* London: Methuen.

Frith, S. (1991). The good, the bad, and the indifferent: Defending popular culture from the populists. *diacritics, 21*, 102–115.

Gadamer, H.-G. (1975). Hermeneutics and social science. *Cultural Hermeneutics, 2*, 307–316.

Gadamer, H.-G. (1992). *Truth and method.* (2nd rev. ed.; J. Weinsheimer & D. G. Marshall, Trans.). New York: Crossroad.

Gergen, K. (1982). *Towards transformation in social knowledge.* New York: Springer-Verlag.

Gergen, K. (1985). The social constructionist movement in modern psychology. *American Psychologist, 40*, 266–275.

Gomery, D. (1993). The centrality of media economics. *Journal of Communication, 43*(3), 190–198.

Goody, J. (1986). *The logic of writing and the organisation of society.* Cambridge, England: Cambridge University Press.

Grice, H. P. (1975). Logic and conversation. In P. Cole & J. Morgan (Eds.), *Syntax and semantics: Vol. 3: Speech acts* (pp. 41–58). New York: Academic .

Grossberg, L. (1993). Can cultural studies find true happiness in communication? *Journal of Communication, 43*(4), 89–97.

Grunig, J. E. (1993). Implications of public relations for other domains of communication. *Journal of Communication, 43*(3), 164–173.

Gurevitch, Z. D. (1989). The other side of dialogue: On making the other strange and the experience of otherness. *American Journal of Sociology, 93*, 1179–1199.

Habermas, J. (1971). *Towards a rational society.* London: Heinemann.

Hammond, S. A. (1996). *The thin book of appreciative inquiry.* Plano, TX: Kodiak Consulting.

Hammond, S. A. & Royal, C. (Eds.). (1998). *Lessons from the field: Applying appreciative inquiry.* Plano, TX: Practical Books Inc.

Harré, R. (1979). *Social being: A theory for social psychology.* Oxford, England: Blackwell.

Harré, R. (1983). *Personal being: A theory for individual psychology.* Oxford, England: Blackwell.

Harré, R. (Ed.). (1986). *The social construction of emotions.* Oxford, England: Blackwell.

Harré, R., & Secord, P. F. (1972). *The explanation of social behaviour.* Totowa, NJ: Littlefield, Adams.

Herbst, S. (1993). History, philosophy and public opinion research. *Journal of Communication, 43*(3), 140–145.

Jacobson, T. L., & Kolluri, S. (1999). Participatory communication as communicative action. In T. L. Jacobson & J. Servaes (Eds.), *Theoretical approaches to participatory communication* (pp. 265–280). Cresskill, NJ: Hampton.

Janik, A., & Toulmin, S. (1973). *Wittgenstein's Vienna.* New York: Simon & Schuster.

Katz, A., & Shotter, J. (1996). Hearing the patient's voice: Towards a 'social poetics' in diagnostic interviews. *Social Science and Medicine, 43*, 919–931.

Katz, A., & Shotter, J. (1997). Resonances from within the practice: Social poetics in a mentorship program. *Concepts and Transformations, 2*, 97–105.

Kavoori, A. P., & Gurevitch, M. (1993). The purebred and the platypus: Disciplinarity and site in mass communication research. *Journal of Communication, 43*(3), 173–181.

Kirschenbaum, H., & Henderson, V. (Eds.). (1989). *Carl Rogers: Dialogues—conversations with Martin Buber, Paul Tillich, B. F. Skinner, Gregory Bateson, Michael Polyani, Rollo May, and others.* Boston: Houghton-Mifflin. Cited in K. Cissna & R. Anderson (1994). Communication and the ground of dialogue. In R. Anderson, K. Cissna, & R. Arnett (Eds.), *The reach of dialogue: Confirmation, voice, and community* (pp. 9–30). Cresskill, NJ: Hampton.

Krippendorff, K. (1989). On the ethics of constructing communication. In B. Dervin, L. Grossberg, B. O'Keefe, & E. Whartella (Eds.), *Rethinking communication: Vol. 1: Paradigm issues* (pp. 66–96). Newbury Park, CA: Sage.

Krippendorff, K. (1993). The past of communication's hoped-for future. *Journal of Communication, 43*(3), 34–44.

Lakoff, G., & Johnson, M. (1980). *Metaphors we live by.* Chicago: University of Chicago Press.

Leeds-Hurwitz, W. (Ed.). (1995). *Social approaches to communication.* New York: Guilford.

Lewin, K. (1951). *Field theory in social science.* New York: Harper & Row.

Lilla, M. (1993). *G. B. Vico: The making of an anti-modern.* Cambridge, MA: Harvard University Press.

Livingstone, S. M. (1993). The rise and fall of audience research: An old story with a new ending. *Journal of Communication, 43*(3), 5–12.

Lock, A. (1978). The emergence of language. In A. Lock (Ed.), *Action, gesture and symbol: The emergence of language* (pp. 1–18). London: Academic.

Locke, J. (1997). *An essay concerning human understanding* (R. Woolhouse, Ed.). London: Penguin. (Original work published 1690)

Lyotard, J.-F. (1984). *The post-modern condition: A report on knowledge.* Manchester, England: Manchester University Press.

Macintyre, A. (1985). *After virtue: A study in moral theory.* London: Duckworth.

MacKenzie-Taylor, M. (1997a). Designing for understanding within a context of rapidly changing information. *Vision Plus Monograph 21E/D.* Vienna: International Institute for Information Design.

MacKenzie-Taylor, M. (1997b). Effective design through conversation: Part 1. *Communication News, 10*(3), 1–4. Canberra: Communication Research Institute of Australia.

MacKenzie-Taylor, M. (1997c). Effective design through conversation: Part 2. *CommunicationNews, 10*(4), 6–9. Canberra: Communication Research Institute of Australia.

McCarthy, T. (1984). *The critical theory of Jürgen Habermas.* Cambridge, England: Polity.

McQuail, D. (1987). *Mass communication theory: An introduction.* London: Sage.

Mead, G. H. (1934). *Mind, self and society: From the standpoint of a social behaviorist.* Chicago: University of Chicago Press.

Mead, G. H. (1938). *The philosophy of the act* (C. W. Morris, Ed.). Chicago: University of Chicago Press.

Melody, W., & Mansell, R. (1983). The debate over critical vs. administrative research: Circularity or challenge. *Journal of Communication, 33*(3), 103–116.

Middleton, D., & Edwards, D. (Eds.). (1990). *Collective remembering.* London: Sage.

Montgomery, B. W,. & Baxter, L. A. (1998). *Dialectical approaches to studying personal relationships.* Mahwah, NJ: Lawrence Erlbaum & Associates.

Morson, G., & Emerson, C. (Eds.). (1989). *Rethinking Bakhtin: Extensions and challenges.* Evanston, IL: Northwestern University Press.

Mühlhäusler, P. (1988). Identifying and mapping the Pidgins and Creoles in the Pacific. In M. Pürtz & R. Dirven (Eds.), *Wheels within wheels* (pp. 287–304). Frankfurt: Verlag.

Parkinson, G. H. R. (1977). The translation theory of understanding. In G. Vesey (Ed.), *Communication and understanding* (pp. 1–19). Sussex, England: Harvester.

Pearce, W. B. (1989). *Communication and the human condition*. Carbondale, II: Southern Illinois University Press.

Pearce, W. B. (1994a). On *"changing the universe": Two ideas and the future of the discipline*. Paper presented at 1994 Institute for Faculty Development: Communication Theory and Research Conference, Hope College, Holland, Michigan.

Pearce, W.B. (1994b). *Interpersonal communication: Making social worlds*. New York: HarperCollins.

Pearce, W. B. (1995). A sailing guide for social constructionists. In W. Leeds-Hurwitz (Ed.), *Social approaches to communication* (pp. 88–113). New York: Guildford.

Pearce. W. B. (1996, July). *Communication, community and democracy*. Keynote address to Australia and New Zealand Communication Association Annual Conference, Brisbane.

Pearce, W. B., & Cronen, V. (1980). *Communication, action and meaning*. New York: Praeger.

Pearce, W. B., & Littlejohn, S. (1997). *Moral conflict: When social worlds collide*. Thousand Oaks, CA: Sage.

Pearce, W. B., & Pearce, K. (1999). Combining passions and abilitites: On becoming virtuosos in dialogue. Unpublsihed manuscript. (To be published in *Southern Commnication Journal, 2000*)

Penman, R. (1987a). Discourse in courts: Cooperation, coercion & coherence. *Discourse Processes, 10,* 201–218.

Penman, R. (1987b). Regulation of discourse in the adversary trial. In C. Wydrzynski (Ed.),*Windsor yearbook of access to justice, vol. VII* (pp. 3–20). Windsor, Canada: University of Windsor.

Penman, R. (1988). Communication re-constructed. *Journal for the Theory of Social Behaviour, 18,* 391–410.

Penman, R. (1990). Communication in the public domain: Whither the citizen's reality? *Australian Journal of Communication 17(3),* 11-21.

Penman, R. (1991). Goals, games & moral orders: A paradoxical case in court? In K. Tracy (Ed.), *Understanding face-to-face interaction* (pp. 21–42). Hillsdale, NJ: Lawrence Erlbaum & Associates.

Penman, R. (1992). Good theory and good practice: An argument in progress. *Communication Theory, 2,* 234–250.

Penman, R. (1993) Conversation is the common theme. *Australian Journal of Communication, 20(3),* 30–43.

Penman, R. (1995). *Participating in research and therapy: What counts as good*. Invited address to Third Dialogical Forum, Rehabilitation Foundation, University of Helsinki.

Penman, R. (1997). The researcher in communication: The primary research position. In J. L. Owen (Ed.), *Context and communication behavior* (pp. 337–351). Reno, NV: Context Press.

Penman, R. (1999, July). *Past-presidents come out: Views on the state of communication studies in Australia*. Paper presented at the Australian & New Zealand Communication Association Conference, University of Western Sydney, Parramatta.

Perlmutter, D. (1997). Manufacturing visions of society and history in textbooks. *Journal of Communication, 47*(3), 68–81.

Peters, J. (1989). John Locke, the individual, and the origin of communication. *Quarterly Journal of Speech, 75*(4), 387–399.

Peters, J. D. (1993). Genealogical notes on "the field". *Journal of Communication, 43*(3), 132–139.

Potter, J., & Litton, I. (1985). Some problems underlying the theory of social representations. *British Journal of Social Psychology, 24,* 81–90.

Pritchard, D., & Hughes, K. (1997). Patterns of deviance in crime news. *Journal of Communication, 47*(3), 49–67.

Rappaport, R. W. (1970). Three dilemnas of action research. *Human Relations, 23,* 499–513.

Reddy, M. (1979). The conduit metaphor. In A. Ortony (Ed.), *Metaphor and thought* (pp. 285–324). London: Cambridge University Press.

Rhee, J. W. (1997). Strategy and issues frames in election campaign coverage: A social cognitive account of framing effects. *Journal of Communication, 47*(3), 26–48.

Rogers, D. (1994). *Dewey on experience: Implications for contemporary communication theory*. Unpublished Masters dissertation, Charles Sturt University, Bathurst, Australia.

Rogers, E. (1982). The empirical and critical schools of communication. In M. Burgoon (Ed.), *Communication yearbook 5* (pp. 125–144). New Brunswick, NJ: Transaction.

Rorty, R. (1980). *Philosophy and the mirror of nature*. Oxford, England: Blackwell.

Rorty, R. (1989). *Contingency, irony & solidarity*. Cambridge, England: Cambridge University Press.

Rosengren, K. E. (1993.) From field to frog ponds. *Journal of Communication, 43*(3), 6–17.

Roth, S. (1997). *Questions and ways of being in therapeutic conversations: Stance and focus of attention*. Unpublished manuscript, Family Institute of Cambridge, Watertown, MA.

Roth, S. (1998). The uncertain path to dialogue: A meditation. In K. Gergen & S. McNamee (Eds.), *Relational responsibility: Resources for sustainable dialogues* (pp. 93–95). Thousand Oaks, CA: Sage.

Roth, S., & Epston, D. (1996a). Consulting the problem about the problematic relationship. In M. F. Hoyt (Ed.), *Constructive therapies: Vol. 2* (pp. 148–162). New York: Guildford.

Roth, S., & Epston, D. (1996b). Developing externalising conversations: An exercise. *Journal of Systemic Therapies, 15*(1), 5–12.

Ryle, G. (1963). *The concept of mind.* Harmondsworth, England: Peregrine.

Salvendy, G. (Ed.). (1987). *Cognitive engineering in the design of human–computer interaction and expert systems, Vol. II.* Amsterdam: Elsevier.

Saul, J. (1992). *Voltaire's bastards: The dictatorship of reason in the West.* London: Sinclair Stevenson.

Scott, J. C. (1998). *Seeing like a state: How certain schemes to improve the human condition have failed.* New Haven: Yale University Press.

Sensat, J. (1979). *Habermas and Marxism.* Beverly Hills, CA: Sage.

Shepherd, G. (1993). Building a discipline of communication. *Journal of Communication, 43,* 83–91.

Shor, I., & Freire, P. (1987). *A pedagogy of liberation: Dialogues on transforming education.* Granby, MA: Bergin & Garvey.

Shotter, J. (1975). *Images of man in psychological research.* London: Methuen.

Shotter, J. (1978). The cultural context of communication studies: Theoretical and methodological issues. In A. Lock (Ed.), *Action, gesture & symbol: The emergence of language* (pp. 43–78). London: Academic.

Shotter, J. (1984.) *Social accountability and selfhood.* Oxford, England: Blackwell.

Shotter, J. (1986). A sense of place: Vico and the social production of social identities. *British Journal of Social Psychology, 24,* 81–90.

Shotter, J. (1987). The social construction of an "us": Problems in accountability and narratology. In R. Burnett, P. McGhee, & D. Clarke (Eds.), *Accounting for personal relationships: Social representations of interpersonal links* (pp. 1–34). London: Methuen.

Shotter, J. (1990). *Knowing of the third kind.* Utrecht: ISOR/University of Utrecht.

Shotter, J. (1993). *Cultural politics of everyday life.* Toronto: University of Toronto Press.

Shotter, J. (1997a, April–May). *Problems with the way of theory.* Paper presented at the ISTP Annual Conference, Berlin.

Shotter, J. (1997b, Spring). *Toward dialogically structured action research: A program of four lectures.* Swedish Institute for Work Life Research, Solna, Stockholm.

Shotter, J. (1997c, March). *Telling of (not about) other voices: 'Real presences' within a text.* Workshop notes for Work Research Institute, Oslo.

Shotter, J. (1998a). The dialogical nature of our inner lives. *Philosophical Explorations, 3,* 185–200.

Shotter, J. (1998b, March). *Against theory and for a social poetic.* Workshop notes for Communication Research Institute of Australia, Canberra, Australia.

Shotter, J., & Gergen, K. J. (Eds.). (1989). *Texts of identity.* London: Sage.

Shusterman, R. (1992). *Pragmatic aesthetics: Living beauty, rethinking art.* Oxford, England: Blackwell.

Sigman, S. (1992). Do social approaches to interpersonal communication constitute a contribution to communication theory? *Communication Theory, 2*(4), 347–356.

Sigman, S. (1995). Introduction: Towards study of the consequentiality (not consequences) of communication. In S. Sigman (Ed.), *The consequentiality of communication* (pp. 1–14). Hillsdale, NJ: Lawrence Erlbaum & Associates.

Simon, A. (1997). Television news and international earthquake relief. *Journal of Communication, 47*(3), 82–93.

Sless, D. (1981). *Learning & visual communication*. London: Croom Helm.

Sless, D. (1986). *In search of semiotics*. London: Croom Helm.

Smythe, D., & Van Dinh, T. (1983). On critical and administrative research: A new critical analysis. *Journal of Communication, 33*(3), 117–127.

Snow, C. (1977). The development of conversations between mothers and babies. *Journal of Child Language, 4*, 1–22.

Spano, S. (1993). *John Locke and the origins of psychological communication*. Paper presented at Speech Communication Association Conference, Miami.

Speake, J. (Ed.). (1979). *A dictionary of philosophy*. London: Pan.

Stewart, J. (Ed.). (1990). *Bridges not walls: A book about interpersonal communication* (5th ed.). New York: Random House.

Stewart, J. (1995). Philosophical features of social approaches to interpersonal communication. In W. Leeds-Hurwitz (Ed.), *Social approaches to communication* (pp. 23–45). New York: Guilford.

Stewart, J., & Zediker, K. (1999, May). *Dialogue as tensional, ethical practice*. Paper presented at the International Communication Association Conference, San Francisco.

Stringer, E. (1996). *Action research: A handbook for practitioners*. Thousand Oaks, CA: Sage.

Tannen, D. (1989). *Talking voices: Repitition, dialogue, and imagery in conversational discourse*. Cambridge, England: Cambridge University Press.

Tinic, S. (1997). United colors and untied meanings: Benetton and the commodification of social issues. *Journal of Communication, 47*(3), 3–25.

Toulmin, S. (1974). *The structure of scientific theories*. Urbana, IL: University of Illinois Press.

Toulmin, S. (1982). The construal of reality: Criticism in modern and post-modern science. *Critical Inquiry, 9*, 93–111.

Toulmin, S. (1990). *Cosmopolis: The hidden agenda of modernity*. Chicago: University of Chicago Press.

Turnbull, S. (1998). Better than literature: Discourses of value and reading crime. *Australian Journal of Communication, 25*(3), 9–24.

Vico, G. (1988). *On the most ancient wisdom of the Italians* (L. M. Palmer, Trans.). Ithaca, NY: Cornell University Press.

Vygotsky, L. (1978). *Mind in society: The development of higher psychological processes* (M. Cole, V. John-Steiner, S. Scribner, & E. Souberman, Eds.). Cambridge, MA: Harvard University Press.

Wheeler, J., Thorne, K,. & Misner, C. (1973). *Gravitation.* San Francisco: Freeman.

White, M. (1993, February). *Conversation with Keynote Speaker,* Discursive Construction of Knowledge Conference, University of Adelaide, South Australia.

Wiley, S. C. (1995, May). *Three or four plateaus: Cultural studies and the detour through philosophy.* Paper presented at the International Communication Association Conference, Albuquerque, NM.

Wittgenstein, L. (1953). *Philosophical investigations.* Oxford, England: Blackwell.

Wittgenstein, L. (1969). *On certainty* (G. E. M. Anscombe & G. von Wright, Eds.; D. Paul & G. E. M. Anscombe, Trans.). Oxford, England: Blackwell.

Wittgenstein, L. (1980). *Culture and value* (G. von Wright, Intro.; P. Winch, Trans.). Oxford, England: Blackwell.

Author index

ᕕᑕ Subject index

◖◗ About the author

Robyn Penman is Executive Director of the Communication Research Institute of Australia, a not-for-profit, independent research organisation which she helped established in 1985; and Adjunct Professor in Communication at the University of Canberra. She received her doctorate in interpersonal communication from the University of Melbourne. She was President of the Australian and New Zealand Communication Association and is a recipient of government and professional society awards for her work on improving communication practices. During her time at the institute she has undertaken practical research and advisory projects for close to 200 public and private sector organizations, working in a wide range of communication contexts. These projects have given her the extensive practical grounding from which her work on practical communication theory and research has been generated. She is the author or editor of four other books and has published scholarly chapters and journal articles on, among other things, communication theory and research, courtroom communication practices, public dialogue and consultation, facework, document comprehensibility and plain English, and environmental matters.